THE XXL
Air Fryer
Cookbook

2022 ~ 2023

Flavorful and Affordable Air Fryer
Recipes for Everyday Air Frying

Hollie Phillips

Table of Contents

Chapter 5 Fish and Seafood — 30

Chapter 6 Vegetables and Sides — 37

INTRODUCTION

Even after being a chef for over 3 years, I was new to air frying until just a few years ago. Once I discovered the air fryer, there was no turning back. It was like a whole new world of cooking and eating experiences opened up to me, so I started experimenting with all sorts of recipes. Some of these recipes came out disgusting, a few were mediocre, but some were absolutely spectacular and completely changed the game of frying.

In this cookery cook, I have brought together the best of my air fryer journey. There are an array of unique tips and tricks throughout the book, so you're in for a treat. Plus, your secret is safe with me if you want to play off the recipes as your own at your next dinner party.

Since the air fryer was invented in 2010, its popularity has steadily increased every year since. Between 2020 and 2021 however, the air fryer market saw a sharp 50% increase. The convenience of air fryers (compared to ovens) and the healthier fried foods they produce are most likely the two biggest reasons for this popularity boom. That combined with the pandemic and more people cooking from home has made for a sharp increase over the last few years.

Here are just a few simple reasons why air frying is awesome:
- Healthier than frying
- They're compact and don't require a lot of space
- They make little to no noise
- Quicker cooking times
- Easy to use
- Less time spent preparing
- Cook almost anything
- Eco-friendly and use less electricity than an oven

I will bet you now that you crave simple, no-fuss recipes. That's why I have created the air fryer cookbook. It's the hassle-free way of cooking meals with easy-to-source ingredients and minimalistic steps that don't take you all day to prepare.

With this cookbook, you will get:
- Plenty of delicious recipes that have been tried, tested and perfected.
- Air fryer tips and tricks to help you master the art of air frying.
- A comprehensive guide on how to choose the best air fryer for your needs as well as how to properly maintain it.

Air frying is a healthier alternative to deep frying as it uses less oil and produces fewer harmful chemicals. Air-fried food is generally less greasy and therefore lighter on the stomach, but with all the flavour you're used to. That's why I love this cooking process so much.

This cookbook is a compilation of my favourite air fryer recipes that I have collected over the last few years. I'm sure these recipes will soon become a staple in your culinary mind - the meals you always fall back on weekly. Move aside Shepherd's pie, we don't have room for dull meals like that anymore.

Chapter 1 Air Fryer 101

Chapter 1 Air Fryer 101

If you're new to air fryers or just looking for a few extra tips on cooking with them then this section is for you. Using an air fryer can be a little tricky to start with. It's a new piece of equipment in the kitchen and like anything else, it will take some getting used to. If you read through this section you'll be ahead of the game and know a little more about air frying than your average cook.

How Do Air Fryers Work

Air fryers work by circulating hot air around the food, essentially 'frying' it without the need for much oil. They move air rapidly over the food at high temperatures, which acts similarly to submerging the food in hot oil.

But, what's the difference between air fryers and conventional ovens in that case? Air fryers and convection ovens are similar in that they both use hot air to cook food. However, Air Fryers cook food faster than convection ovens and make food extra crispy due to the heat intensity inside.

Air fryers circulate hot air around the food at high speed, creating a crispy outer layer while keeping the inside juicy. This is due to the Maillard reaction, which is a chemical reaction that occurs between amino acids and sugars when heated. The Maillard reaction is the reason why foods become golden brown and crispy.

To put it in layman's terms, you know the crispy crust on seared steak? That's because of the cooking process that causes the Maillard reaction to occur. Air fryers essentially cause this reaction to occur, but differently to conventional cooking methods that require lots of oil, they use air instead.

5 Features of Air Fryer

Less Fat

Air fryers use little to no oil, making them a healthier option than deep fryers. All you need to do is add around 1 tablespoon of oil and the results are just as though the food has been deep-fried. By utilising this method, you can cut down your calorie intake by 70% to 80%, as well as significantly reduce the amount of fat in your food. Additionally, it might also help mitigate other harmful effects related to oil frying. Crispy on the Outside, juicy on the inside with minimal oil and all the tastiness as expected.

Faster Meals

Air fryers can cook food up to 50% faster than traditional methods. This is because the hot air circulates the food at a high speed, cooking it evenly on all sides but giving the heat intensity as though you would submerge the food in oil. Plus with the paddle-type versions, you can set and forget so you can go and

do other things while the fryer works its magic, without you having to check for burning every 5 minutes.

More Meal Choices

Air fryers can do more than just frying food. You can also use them to bake, grill, and roast food. If you didn't already have a deep-fat fryer, then an air fryer will open up the possibility of cooking lots of different recipes that would usually need some sort of fat fryer. Fish and chips? Yep! Crispy chicken nuggets? Yep!

Less Energy

Air fryers use less energy than other cooking methods, such as ovens. On average, air fryers use 1500 watts of energy as opposed to the 2300 kWh that is necessary to run a conventional oven in your home. If you break it down, this means that an air fryer uses about half of the power/energy as a regular oven would. Air fryers also don't heat your kitchen as much as an oven would, making them perfect for summer cooking.

Enough Capacity

Air fryers come in a variety of sizes, so you can find one that fits your needs. The average air fryer can cook enough food for two to four people. If you have a larger family, you can find air fryers that can accommodate six to eight people. Obviously the larger unit you need the more expensive they tend to be, but there are some great choices of different sizes.

Different Types of Air Fryers

Basket Air Fryers

An air fryer with a basket shape allows you to cook your food within a compartmentalised container. There are small holes in the basket so that air can flow freely and heat the food accordingly. This avoids your meal from sitting in excess oil too. You can find this style in a variety of shapes and sizes to suit your capacity and cooking requirements.

A great basket air fryer choice is the Tower Family Size Air Fryer. It has 4.3 litres of capacity so that you can easily cook a meal and have enough for the whole family. With this model, I have found that the food is always extra crispy when cooked.

Air Fryers Ovens

Oven air fryers can bake, roast, grill, toast, fry, and broil food. They are multifunctional cooking tools that offer a range of different cooking methods. Oven air fryers are unique in the sense that they have racks so you can do multiple layers of food.

With an oven air fryer, the door is transparent glass so you can see the cooking process easily from the outside, unlike most other air fryer types. You can also clean their components in the dishwasher which some other types do not allow.

Breville Halo Rotisserie Air Fryer is an excellent oven air fryer. It has 10 litres of capacity and 3 levels of cooking. This is certainly the best option if you have a large family to feed.

Cylindrical Basket Air Fryer

Two baskets are present in a cylindrical air fryer. The fryer uses a fan to circulate the hot air and this allows for the fryer to heat up in as little as 2 minutes. This type of fryer is small and compact plus there is no residual heat so you can use them during hot summer days without overheating the kitchen.

The Tefal ActiFry Genius is a great example of a cylindrical air fryer. It can cook up to 8 portions at once, has 54 smart programs to cook all parts of a meal plus 9 smart auto programs to set and forget.

Pressure Air Fryers

Again a combo of a pressure cooker and air fryer. The tenderness of cooking with pressure and the crispy brown exterior that air fryers are famous for. The lid seals securely to build up pressure within the cooker. This allows for a faster cooking process too.

The famous Ninja air fryers are top of the market and the Ninja Foodi Multi-Cooker pressure cooker and air fryer is at the pinnacle of Ninjas models. The fryer has 9 ways to cook, including pressure, air fryer, slow cook and grill. This one is ideal for up to 6 people.

Halogen Air Fryers

Particularly useful for its glass exterior so that you can see where the cooking process is up to when making a meal. It's a type of cooking that utilises a heating element and a powerful fan. The strong fan will rapidly move the extremely hot air produced by the heating element throughout the air fryer. This circulation of super-hot air is what cooks your meal.

The Tower T14001 Health Halogen air fryer only uses 1300W to cook so the cost of running this thing is pennies. It has a huge

capacity of 17 litres so would even be fit to use for a dinner part. There are multiple cooking options and like with all halogen cookers, you can see the cooking process in action.

Air Fryer Cooking Tips

When cooking with an air fryer it's important to remember a few key things:

- ♦ Air fryers work best when used for small batches of food. This ensures that each piece of food gets cooked evenly.
- ♦ Preheat your air fryer before cooking. This helps the food cook more evenly throughout.
- ♦ Cut your food into even pieces. This helps the food cook evenly and prevents it from sticking to the basket.
- ♦ Shake or stir your food halfway through cooking. This helps distribute the heat and prevents burning.
- ♦ Use a cooking spray or oil to prevent sticking and ensure even cooking.
- ♦ Check your food often towards the end of cooking. Air fryers can cook food quickly, so you don't want it to burn.
- ♦ Add water to the fryer when cooking fatty foods so that the grease doesn't get too hot and start smoking.
- ♦ Don't overcrowd the basket so your food gets that lovely crisp all over. This is important: resist the urge to overcrowd the basket. If you do, foods won't crisp and brown evenly, and it'll take longer overall.
- ♦ To ensure that your foods cook evenly, remember to flip it over midway through the cooking process. This is exactly like if you're using a grill or skillet.
- ♦ Check the air fryer frequently to ensure that it is cooked. One of the greatest features of air fryers is that you may open the drawer as often as you like (within reason) to monitor how the cooking process is progressing. For most air fryers, removing the basket will not pause or change the heating or timing functions.
- ♦ Toothpicks can be used to keep the food in place. The fan from the air fryer will occasionally pick up light items and fling them about. So, toothpicks should be used to hold down delicacies (such as sticking a sandwich together).

Care & Cleaning

When it comes to caring and cleaning, air fryers are pretty low maintenance. The majority of air fryers have dishwasher-safe parts, so you can simply pop them in the dishwasher when they need to be cleaned. Some air fryers have a nonstick coating, which makes them even easier to clean although this may not be dishwasher-proof.

If your air fryer doesn't have dishwasher-safe parts, then you can clean it by hand. Simply remove the basket and wash it with soap and water. You can wipe down the inside of the air fryer with a damp cloth. Be sure to unplug the air fryer before cleaning it. For the outside, you may find some residual fat building up. The best way to remove this is by spraying the kitchen cleaner directly onto the fryer and then wiping it with a damp cloth.

Air Fryer Q&A

Q: Can I put aluminium foil in an air fryer?

A: Yes, you can put aluminium foil in an air fryer. You'll need to use a small piece of foil so that it doesn't touch the sides or bottom of the air fryer. Place the food on top of the foil and cook as usual.

Q: What can't you cook in an air fryer?

A: There are a few things that you shouldn't cook in an Air Fryer, such as raw chicken breasts, whole fish, and large cuts of meat. These items are better suited for other cooking methods, such as grilling or baking.

Q: How long do Air Fried foods last?

A: Air Fried foods will last for two to three days in the refrigerator. Be sure to store them in an airtight container so that they don't dry out.

Q: What's the best way to reheat Air Fried foods?

A: The best way to reheat Air Fried foods is in the Air Fryer. Simply place the food in the Air Fryer and cook for a few minutes until it's heated through. You can also reheat Air Fried foods in the microwave, but they won't be as crisp.

Q: Can I Air Fry frozen foods?

A: Yes, you can Air Fry frozen foods. You'll need to cook them for a longer period of time than fresh food. Be sure to check the Air Fryer manual for specific cooking times.

Q: Can I Air Fry foods that are breaded?

A: Yes, you can Air Fry foods that are breaded. The breading will help to create a crispy outside. Make sure to coat the food evenly with breading and cook it for the recommended amount of time.

Chapter 2 Breakfasts

Chapter 2 Breakfasts

Spinach Omelet

Prep time: 5 minutes | Cook time: 12 minutes | Serves 2

4 large eggs
350 ml chopped fresh spinach leaves
2 tablespoons peeled and chopped brown onion
2 tablespoons salted butter, melted
120 ml shredded mild Cheddar cheese
¼ teaspoon salt

1. In an ungreased round nonstick baking dish, whisk eggs. Stir in spinach, onion, butter, Cheddar, and salt.
2. Place dish into air fryer basket. Adjust the temperature to 160°C and bake for 12 minutes. Omelet will be done when browned on the top and firm in the middle.
3. Slice in half and serve warm on two medium plates.

Strawberry Tarts

Prep time: 15 minutes | Cook time: 10 minutes | Serves 6

2 refrigerated piecrusts
120 ml strawberry preserves
1 teaspoon cornflour
Cooking oil spray
120 ml low-fat vanilla yoghurt
30 g cream cheese, at room temperature
3 tablespoons icing sugar
Rainbow sprinkles, for decorating

1. Place the piecrusts on a flat surface. Using a knife or pizza cutter, cut each piecrust into 3 rectangles, for 6 total. Discard any unused dough from the piecrust edges.
2. In a small bowl, stir together the preserves and cornflour. Mix well, ensuring there are no lumps of cornflour remaining.
3. Scoop 1 tablespoon of the strawberry mixture onto the top half of each piece of piecrust.
4. Fold the bottom of each piece up to enclose the filling. Using the back of a fork, press along the edges of each tart to seal.
5. Insert the crisper plate into the basket and the basket into the unit. Preheat the unit by selecting BAKE, setting the temperature to 192°C, and setting the time to 3 minutes. Select START/STOP to begin.
6. Once the unit is preheated, spray the crisper plate with cooking oil. Working in batches, spray the breakfast tarts with cooking oil and place them into the basket in a single layer. Do not stack the tarts.
7. Select BAKE, set the temperature to 192°C, and set the time to 10 minutes. Select START/STOP to begin.

8. When the cooking is complete, the tarts should be light golden brown. Let the breakfast tarts cool fully before removing them from the basket.
9. Repeat steps 5, 6, 7, and 8 for the remaining breakfast tarts.
10. In a small bowl, stir together the yoghurt, cream cheese, and icing sugar. Spread the breakfast tarts with the frosting and top with sprinkles.

Bacon, Broccoli and Cheese Bread Pudding

Prep time: 30 minutes | Cook time: 48 minutes | Serves 2 to 4

230 g thick cut bacon, cut into ¼-inch pieces
700 ml brioche bread or rolls, cut into ½-inch cubes
3 eggs
235 ml milk
½ teaspoon salt
freshly ground black pepper
235 ml frozen broccoli florets, thawed and chopped
350 ml grated Swiss cheese

1. Preheat the air fryer to 204°C.
2. Air fry the bacon for 6 to 10 minutes until crispy, shaking the basket a few times while it cooks to help it cook evenly. Remove the bacon and set it aside on a paper towel.
3. Air fry the brioche bread cubes for 2 minutes to dry and toast lightly. (If your brioche is a few days old and slightly stale, you can omit this step.)
4. Butter a cake pan. Combine all the ingredients in a large bowl and toss well. Transfer the mixture to the buttered cake pan, cover with aluminum foil and refrigerate the bread pudding overnight, or for at least 8 hours.
5. Remove the casserole from the refrigerator an hour before you plan to cook, and let it sit on the countertop to come to room temperature.
6. Preheat the air fryer to 166°C. Transfer the covered cake pan, to the basket of the air fryer, lowering the dish into the basket using a sling made of aluminum foil (fold a piece of aluminum foil into a strip about 2-inches wide by 24-inches long). Fold the ends of the aluminum foil over the top of the dish before returning the basket to the air fryer. Air fry for 20 minutes. Remove the foil and air fry for an additional 20 minutes. If the top starts to brown a little too much before the custard has set, simply return the foil to the pan. The bread pudding has cooked through when a skewer inserted into the center comes out clean.

Easy Sausage Pizza

Prep time: 10 minutes | Cook time: 6 minutes | Serves 4

2 tablespoons ketchup
1 pitta bread
80 ml sausage meat

230 g Mozzarella cheese
1 teaspoon garlic powder
1 tablespoon olive oil

1. Preheat the air fryer to 172°C.
2. Spread the ketchup over the pitta bread.
3. Top with the sausage meat and cheese. Sprinkle with the garlic powder and olive oil.
4. Put the pizza in the air fryer basket and bake for 6 minutes.
5. Serve warm.

Chimichanga Breakfast Burrito

Prep time: 10 minutes | Cook time: 10 minutes | Serves 2

2 large (10- to 12-inch) flour tortillas
120 ml canned refried beans (pinto or black work equally well)
4 large eggs, cooked scrambled

4 corn tortilla chips, crushed
120 ml grated chili cheese
12 pickled jalapeño slices
1 tablespoon vegetable oil
Guacamole, salsa, and sour cream, for serving (optional)

1. Place the tortillas on a work surface and divide the refried beans between them, spreading them in a rough rectangle in the center of the tortillas. Top the beans with the scrambled eggs, crushed chips, cheese, and jalapeños. Fold one side over the fillings, then fold in each short side and roll up the rest of the way like a burrito.
2. Brush the outside of the burritos with the oil, then transfer to the air fryer, seam-side down. Air fry at 176°C until the tortillas are browned and crisp and the filling is warm throughout, about 10 minutes.
3. Transfer the chimichangas to plates and serve warm with guacamole, salsa, and sour cream, if you like.

Bacon, Egg, and Cheese Roll Ups

Prep time: 15 minutes | Cook time: 15 minutes | Serves 4

2 tablespoons unsalted butter
60 ml chopped onion
½ medium green pepper, seeded and chopped
6 large eggs

12 slices bacon
235 ml shredded sharp Cheddar cheese
120 ml mild salsa, for dipping

1. In a medium skillet over medium heat, melt butter. Add onion and pepper to the skillet and sauté until fragrant and onions are translucent, about 3 minutes.
2. Whisk eggs in a small bowl and pour into skillet. Scramble eggs with onions and peppers until fluffy and fully cooked, about 5 minutes. Remove from heat and set aside.
3. On work surface, place three slices of bacon side by side, overlapping about ¼ inch. Place 60 ml scrambled eggs in a heap on the side closest to you and sprinkle 60 ml cheese on top of the eggs.
4. Tightly roll the bacon around the eggs and secure the seam with a toothpick if necessary. Place each roll into the air fryer basket.
5. Adjust the temperature to 176°C and air fry for 15 minutes. Rotate the rolls halfway through the cooking time.
6. Bacon will be brown and crispy when completely cooked. Serve immediately with salsa for dipping.

Baked Egg and Mushroom Cups

Prep time: 5 minutes | Cook time: 15 minutes | Serves 6

Olive oil cooking spray
6 large eggs
1 garlic clove, minced
½ teaspoon salt
½ teaspoon black pepper

Pinch red pepper flakes
230 g baby mushrooms, sliced
235 ml fresh baby spinach
2 spring onions, white parts and green parts, diced

1. Preheat the air fryer to 160°C. Lightly coat the inside of six silicone muffin cups or a six-cup muffin tin with olive oil cooking spray.
2. In a large bowl, beat the eggs, garlic, salt, pepper, and red pepper flakes for 1 to 2 minutes, or until well combined.
3. Fold in the mushrooms, spinach, and spring onions.
4. Divide the mixture evenly among the muffin cups.
5. Place into the air fryer and bake for 12 to 15 minutes, or until the eggs are set.
6. Remove and allow to cool for 5 minutes before serving.

Buffalo Egg Cups

Prep time: 10 minutes | Cook time: 15 minutes | Serves 2

4 large eggs
60 g full-fat cream cheese
2 tablespoons buffalo sauce

120 ml shredded sharp Cheddar cheese

1. Crack eggs into two ramekins.
2. In a small microwave-safe bowl, mix cream cheese, buffalo sauce, and Cheddar. Microwave for 20 seconds and then stir. Place a spoonful into each ramekin on top of the eggs.
3. Place ramekins into the air fryer basket.
4. Adjust the temperature to 160°C and bake for 15 minutes.
5. Serve warm.

Breakfast Pitta

Prep time: 5 minutes | Cook time: 6 minutes | Serves 2

1 wholemeal pitta
2 teaspoons olive oil
½ shallot, diced
¼ teaspoon garlic, minced
1 large egg

¼ teaspoon dried oregano
¼ teaspoon dried thyme
⅛ teaspoon salt
2 tablespoons shredded
Parmesan cheese

1. Preheat the air fryer to 192ºC.
2. Brush the top of the pitta with olive oil, then spread the diced shallot and minced garlic over the pitta.
3. Crack the egg into a small bowl or ramekin, and season it with oregano, thyme, and salt.
4. Place the pitta into the air fryer basket, and gently pour the egg onto the top of the pitta. Sprinkle with cheese over the top.
5. Bake for 6 minutes.
6. Allow to cool for 5 minutes before cutting into pieces for serving.

Apple Cider Doughnut Holes

Prep time: 10 minutes | Cook time: 6 minutes | Makes 10 mini doughnuts

Doughnut Holes:
350 ml plain flour
2 tablespoons granulated sugar
2 teaspoons baking powder
1 teaspoon baking soda
½ teaspoon coarse or flaky salt
Pinch of freshly grated nutmeg
60 ml plus 2 tablespoons buttermilk, chilled
2 tablespoons apple cider or

apple juice, chilled
1 large egg, lightly beaten
Vegetable oil, for brushing
Glaze:
120 ml icing sugar
2 tablespoons unsweetened applesauce
¼ teaspoon vanilla extract
Pinch of coarse or flaky salt

1. Make the doughnut holes: In a bowl, whisk together the flour, granulated sugar, baking powder, baking soda, salt, and nutmeg until smooth. Add the buttermilk, cider, and egg and stir with a small rubber spatula or spoon until the dough just comes together.
2. Using a 28 g ice cream scoop or 2 tablespoons, scoop and drop 10 balls of dough into the air fryer basket, spaced evenly apart, and brush the tops lightly with oil. Air fry at 176ºC until the doughnut holes are golden brown and fluffy, about 6 minutes. Transfer the doughnut holes to a wire rack to cool completely.
3. Make the glaze: In a small bowl, stir together the powdered sugar, applesauce, vanilla, and salt until smooth.
4. Dip the tops of the doughnuts holes in the glaze, then let stand until the glaze sets before serving. If you're impatient and want warm doughnuts, have the glaze ready to go while the doughnuts cook, then use the glaze as a dipping sauce for the warm doughnuts, fresh out of the air fryer.

Turkey Breakfast Sausage Patties

Prep time: 5 minutes | Cook time: 10 minutes | Serves 4

1 tablespoon chopped fresh thyme
1 tablespoon chopped fresh sage
1¼ teaspoons coarse or flaky salt
1 teaspoon chopped fennel seeds
¾ teaspoon smoked paprika
½ teaspoon onion granules

½ teaspoon garlic powder
⅛ teaspoon crushed red pepper flakes
⅛ teaspoon freshly ground black pepper
450 g lean turkey mince
120 ml finely minced sweet apple (peeled)

1. Thoroughly combine the thyme, sage, salt, fennel seeds, paprika, onion granules, garlic powder, red pepper flakes, and black pepper in a medium bowl.
2. Add the turkey mince and apple and stir until well incorporated. Divide the mixture into 8 equal portions and shape into patties with your hands, each about ¼ inch thick and 3 inches in diameter.
3. Preheat the air fryer to 204ºC.
4. Place the patties in the air fryer basket in a single layer. You may need to work in batches to avoid overcrowding.
5. Air fry for 5 minutes. Flip the patties and air fry for 5 minutes, or until the patties are nicely browned and cooked through.
6. Remove from the basket to a plate and repeat with the remaining patties.
7. Serve warm.

Quick and Easy Blueberry Muffins

Prep time: 10 minutes | Cook time: 12 minutes | Makes 8 muffins

315 ml flour
120 ml sugar
2 teaspoons baking powder
¼ teaspoon salt
80 ml rapeseed oil

1 egg
120 ml milk
160 ml blueberries, fresh or frozen and thawed

1. Preheat the air fryer to 166ºC.
2. In a medium bowl, stir together flour, sugar, baking powder, and salt.
3. In a separate bowl, combine oil, egg, and milk and mix well.
4. Add egg mixture to dry ingredients and stir just until moistened.
5. Gently stir in the blueberries.
6. Spoon batter evenly into parchment paper-lined muffin cups.
7. Put 4 muffin cups in air fryer basket and bake for 12 minutes or until tops spring back when touched lightly.
8. Repeat previous step to bake remaining muffins.
9. Serve immediately.

Wholemeal Banana-Walnut Bread

Prep time: 10 minutes | Cook time: 23 minutes | Serves 6

Olive oil cooking spray
2 ripe medium bananas
1 large egg
60 ml non-fat plain Greek yoghurt
60 ml olive oil
½ teaspoon vanilla extract
2 tablespoons honey
235 ml wholemeal flour
¼ teaspoon salt
¼ teaspoon baking soda
½ teaspoon ground cinnamon
60 ml chopped walnuts

1. Preheat the air fryer to 182°C. Lightly coat the inside of a 8-by-4-inch loaf pan with olive oil cooking spray. (Or use two 5 ½-by-3-inch loaf pans.)
2. In a large bowl, mash the bananas with a fork. Add the egg, yoghurt, olive oil, vanilla, and honey. Mix until well combined and mostly smooth.
3. Sift the wholemeal flour, salt, baking soda, and cinnamon into the wet mixture, then stir until just combined. Do not overmix.
4. Gently fold in the walnuts.
5. Pour into the prepared loaf pan and spread to distribute evenly.
6. Place the loaf pan in the air fryer basket and bake for 20 to 23 minutes, or until golden brown on top and a toothpick inserted into the center comes out clean.
7. Allow to cool for 5 minutes before serving.

Double-Dipped Mini Cinnamon Biscuits

Prep time: 15 minutes | Cook time: 13 minutes | Makes 8 biscuits

475 ml blanched almond flour
120 ml liquid or powdered sweetener
1 teaspoon baking powder
½ teaspoon fine sea salt
60 ml plus 2 tablespoons (¾ stick) very cold unsalted butter
60 ml unsweetened, unflavoured almond milk
1 large egg
1 teaspoon vanilla extract
3 teaspoons ground cinnamon
Glaze:
120 ml powdered sweetener
60 ml double cream or unsweetened, unflavoured almond milk

1. Preheat the air fryer to 176°C. Line a pie pan that fits into your air fryer with parchment paper.
2. In a medium-sized bowl, mix together the almond flour, sweetener (if powdered; do not add liquid sweetener), baking powder, and salt. Cut the butter into ½-inch squares, then use a hand mixer to work the butter into the dry ingredients. When you are done, the mixture should still have chunks of butter.
3. In a small bowl, whisk together the almond milk, egg, and vanilla extract (if using liquid sweetener, add it as well) until blended.

Using a fork, stir the wet ingredients into the dry ingredients until large clumps form. Add the cinnamon and use your hands to swirl it into the dough.
4. Form the dough into sixteen 1-inch balls and place them on the prepared pan, spacing them about ½ inch apart. (If you're using a smaller air fryer, work in batches if necessary.) Bake in the air fryer until golden, 10 to 13 minutes. Remove from the air fryer and let cool on the pan for at least 5 minutes.
5. While the biscuits bake, make the glaze: Place the powdered sweetener in a small bowl and slowly stir in the heavy cream with a fork.
6. When the biscuits have cooled somewhat, dip the tops into the glaze, allow it to dry a bit, and then dip again for a thick glaze.
7. Serve warm or at room temperature. Store unglazed biscuits in an airtight container in the refrigerator for up to 3 days or in the freezer for up to a month. Reheat in a preheated 176°C air fryer for 5 minutes, or until warmed through, and dip in the glaze as instructed above.

Homemade Cherry Breakfast Tarts

Prep time: 15 minutes | Cook time: 20 minutes | Serves 6

Tarts:
2 refrigerated piecrusts
80 ml cherry preserves
1 teaspoon cornflour
Cooking oil
Frosting:
120 ml vanilla yoghurt
30 g cream cheese
1 teaspoon stevia
Rainbow sprinkles

Make the Tarts 1. Place the piecrusts on a flat surface. Using a knife or pizza cutter, cut each piecrust into 3 rectangles, for 6 total. (I discard the unused dough left from slicing the edges.)
2. In a small bowl, combine the preserves and cornflour. Mix well.
3. Scoop 1 tablespoon of the preserves mixture onto the top half of each piece of piecrust.
4. Fold the bottom of each piece up to close the tart. Using the back of a fork, press along the edges of each tart to seal.
5. Spray the breakfast tarts with cooking oil and place them in the air fryer. I do not recommend stacking the breakfast tarts. They will stick together if stacked. You may need to prepare them in two batches. Bake at 375°F for 10 minutes.
6. Allow the breakfast tarts to cool fully before removing from the air fryer.
7. If necessary, repeat steps 5 and 6 for the remaining breakfast tarts. Make the Frosting
8. In a small bowl, combine the yoghurt, cream cheese, and stevia. Mix well.
9. Spread the breakfast tarts with frosting and top with sprinkles, and serve.

Veggie Frittata

Prep time: 7 minutes | Cook time: 21 to 23 minutes | Serves 2

Avocado oil spray
60 ml diced red onion
60 ml diced red pepper
60 ml finely chopped broccoli
4 large eggs

85 g shredded sharp Cheddar cheese, divided
½ teaspoon dried thyme
Sea salt and freshly ground black pepper, to taste

1. Spray a pan well with oil. Put the onion, pepper, and broccoli in the pan, place the pan in the air fryer, and set to 176ºC. Bake for 5 minutes.
2. While the vegetables cook, beat the eggs in a medium bowl. Stir in half of the cheese, and season with the thyme, salt, and pepper.
3. Add the eggs to the pan and top with the remaining cheese. Set the air fryer to 176ºC. Bake for 16 to 18 minutes, until cooked through.

Tomato and Cheddar Rolls

Prep time: 30 minutes | Cook time: 25 minutes | Makes 12 rolls

4 plum tomatoes
½ clove garlic, minced
1 tablespoon olive oil
¼ teaspoon dried thyme
Salt and freshly ground black pepper, to taste
1 L plain flour
1 teaspoon active dry yeast

2 teaspoons sugar
2 teaspoons salt
1 tablespoon olive oil
235 ml grated Cheddar cheese, plus more for sprinkling at the end
350 ml water

1. Cut the tomatoes in half, remove the seeds with your fingers and transfer to a bowl. Add the garlic, olive oil, dried thyme, salt and freshly ground black pepper and toss well.
2. Preheat the air fryer to 200ºC.
3. Place the tomatoes, cut side up in the air fryer basket and air fry for 10 minutes. The tomatoes should just start to brown. Shake the basket to redistribute the tomatoes, and air fry for another 5 to 10 minutes at 166ºC until the tomatoes are no longer juicy. Let the tomatoes cool and then rough chop them.
4. Combine the flour, yeast, sugar and salt in the bowl of a stand mixer. Add the olive oil, chopped roasted tomatoes and Cheddar cheese to the flour mixture and start to mix using the dough hook attachment. As you're mixing, add 300 ml of the water, mixing until the dough comes together. Continue to knead the dough with the dough hook for another 10 minutes, adding enough water to the dough to get it to the right consistency.
5. Transfer the dough to an oiled bowl, cover with a clean kitchen towel and let it rest and rise until it has doubled in volume, about 1 to 2 hours. Then, divide the dough into 12 equal portions. Roll each

portion of dough into a ball. Lightly coat each dough ball with oil and let the dough balls rest and rise a second time, covered lightly with plastic wrap for 45 minutes. (Alternately, you can place the rolls in the refrigerator overnight and take them out 2 hours before you bake them.)
6. Preheat the air fryer to 182ºC.
7. Spray the dough balls and the air fryer basket with a little olive oil. Place three rolls at a time in the basket and bake for 10 minutes. Add a little grated Cheddar cheese on top of the rolls for the last 2 minutes of air frying for an attractive finish.

Red Pepper and Feta Frittata

Prep time: 10 minutes | Cook time: 20 minutes | Serves 4

Olive oil cooking spray
8 large eggs
1 medium red pepper, diced
½ teaspoon salt

½ teaspoon black pepper
1 garlic clove, minced
120 ml feta, divided

1. Preheat the air fryer to 182ºC. Lightly coat the inside of a 6-inch round cake pan with olive oil cooking spray.
2. In a large bowl, beat the eggs for 1 to 2 minutes, or until well combined.
3. Add the red pepper, salt, black pepper, and garlic to the eggs, and mix together until the red pepper is distributed throughout.
4. Fold in 60 ml the feta cheese.
5. Pour the egg mixture into the prepared cake pan, and sprinkle the remaining 60 ml feta over the top.
6. Place into the air fryer and bake for 18 to 20 minutes, or until the eggs are set in the center.
7. Remove from the air fryer and allow to cool for 5 minutes before serving.

Sausage and Cheese Balls

Prep time: 10 minutes | Cook time: 12 minutes | Makes 16 balls

450 g pork sausage meat, removed from casings
120 ml shredded Cheddar cheese

30 g full-fat cream cheese, softened
1 large egg

1. Mix all ingredients in a large bowl. Form into sixteen (1-inch) balls. Place the balls into the air fryer basket.
2. Adjust the temperature to 204ºC and air fry for 12 minutes.
3. Shake the basket two or three times during cooking. Sausage balls will be browned on the outside and have an internal temperature of at least 64ºC when completely cooked.
4. Serve warm.

Cheddar-Ham-Corn Muffins

Prep time: 10 minutes | Cook time: 6 to 8 minutes per batch | Makes 8 muffins

180 ml cornmeal/polenta
60 ml flour
1½ teaspoons baking powder
¼ teaspoon salt
1 egg, beaten

2 tablespoons rapeseed oil
120 ml milk
120 ml shredded sharp Cheddar cheese
120 ml diced ham
8 foil muffin cups, liners removed and sprayed with cooking spray

1. Preheat the air fryer to 200ºC.
2. In a medium bowl, stir together the cornmeal, flour, baking powder, and salt.
3. Add egg, oil, and milk to dry ingredients and mix well.
4. Stir in shredded cheese and diced ham.
5. Divide batter among the muffin cups.
6. Place 4 filled muffin cups in air fryer basket and bake for 5 minutes.
7. Reduce temperature to 166ºC and bake for 1 to 2 minutes or until toothpick inserted in center of muffin comes out clean.
8. Repeat steps 6 and 7 to cook remaining muffins.

Chapter 3 Poultry

Cheese-Encrusted Chicken Tenderloins with Peanuts

Prep time: 10 minutes | Cook time: 25 minutes | Serves 4

45 g grated Parmesan cheese
½ teaspoon garlic powder
1 teaspoon red pepper flakes
Sea salt and ground black pepper, to taste

2 tablespoons peanut oil
680 g chicken tenderloins
2 tablespoons peanuts, roasted and roughly chopped
Cooking spray

1. Preheat the air fryer to 180°C. Spritz the air fryer basket with cooking spray.
2. Combine the Parmesan cheese, garlic powder, red pepper flakes, salt, black pepper, and peanut oil in a large bowl. Stir to mix well.
3. Dip the chicken tenderloins in the cheese mixture, then press to coat well. Shake the excess off.
4. Transfer the chicken tenderloins in the air fryer basket. Air fry for 12 minutes or until well browned. Flip the tenderloin halfway through. You may need to work in batches to avoid overcrowding.
5. Transfer the chicken tenderloins on a large plate and top with roasted peanuts before serving.

Bacon Lovers' Stuffed Chicken

Prep time: 15 minutes | Cook time: 10 minutes | Serves 4

4 (140 g) boneless, skinless chicken breasts, pounded to ¼ inch thick
2 (150 g) packages Boursin cheese (or Kite Hill brand chive cream cheese style spread,

softened, for dairy-free)
8 slices thin-cut bacon or beef bacon
Sprig of fresh coriander, for garnish (optional)

1. Spray the air fryer basket with avocado oil. Preheat the air fryer to 200°C.
2. Place one of the chicken breasts on a cutting board. With a sharp knife held parallel to the cutting board, make a 1-inch-wide incision at the top of the breast. Carefully cut into the breast to form a large pocket, leaving a ½-inch border along the sides and bottom. Repeat with the other 3 chicken breasts.
3. Snip the corner of a large resealable plastic bag to form a ¾-inch hole. Place the Boursin cheese in the bag and pipe the cheese into the pockets in the chicken breasts, dividing the cheese evenly among them.
4. Wrap 2 slices of bacon around each chicken breast and secure

the ends with toothpicks. Place the bacon-wrapped chicken in the air fryer basket and air fry until the bacon is crisp and the chicken's internal temperature reaches 76°C, about 18 to 20 minutes, flipping after 10 minutes. Garnish with a sprig of coriander before serving, if desired.
5. Store leftovers in an airtight container in the refrigerator for up to 4 days. Reheat in a preheated 200°C air fryer for 5 minutes, or until warmed through.

Easy Chicken Nachos

Prep time: 5 minutes | Cook time: 5 minutes | Serves 8

Oil, for spraying
420 g shredded cooked chicken
1 (30 g) package ranch seasoning
60 g sour cream

55 g corn tortilla chips
75 g bacon bits
235 g shredded Cheddar cheese
1 tablespoon chopped spring onions

1. Line the air fryer basket with parchment and spray lightly with oil.
2. In a small bowl, mix together the chicken, ranch seasoning, and sour cream.
3. Place the tortilla chips in the prepared basket and top with the chicken mixture. Add the bacon bits, Cheddar cheese, and spring onions.
4. Air fry at 220°C for 3 to 5 minutes, or until heated through and the cheese is melted.

Chipotle Aioli Wings

Prep time: 5 minutes | Cook time: 25 minutes | Serves 6

900 g bone-in chicken wings
½ teaspoon salt
¼ teaspoon ground black pepper

2 tablespoons mayonnaise
2 teaspoons chipotle powder
2 tablespoons lemon juice

1. In a large bowl, toss wings in salt and pepper, then place into ungreased air fryer basket. Adjust the temperature to 200°C and air fry for 25 minutes, shaking the basket twice while cooking. Wings will be done when golden and have an internal temperature of at least 76°C.
2. In a small bowl, whisk together mayonnaise, chipotle powder, and lemon juice. Place cooked wings into a large serving bowl and drizzle with aioli. Toss to coat. Serve warm.

One-Dish Chicken and Rice

Prep time: 10 minutes | Cook time: 40 minutes | Serves 4

190 g long-grain white rice, rinsed and drained
120 g cut frozen green beans (do not thaw)
1 tablespoon minced fresh ginger

3 cloves garlic, minced
1 tablespoon toasted sesame oil
1 teaspoon kosher salt
1 teaspoon black pepper
450 g chicken wings, preferably drumettes

1. In a baking pan, combine the rice, green beans, ginger, garlic, sesame oil, salt, and pepper. Stir to combine. Place the chicken wings on top of the rice mixture.
2. Cover the pan with foil. Make a long slash in the foil to allow the pan to vent steam. Place the pan in the air fryer basket. Set the air fryer to (190ºC for 30 minutes.
3. Remove the foil. Set the air fryer to 200ºC for 10 minutes, or until the wings have browned and rendered fat into the rice and vegetables, turning the wings halfway through the cooking time.

Gochujang Chicken Wings

Prep time: 15 minutes | Cook time: 25 minutes | Serves 4

Wings:
900 g chicken wings
1 teaspoon kosher salt
1 teaspoon black pepper or gochugaru (Korean red pepper)
Sauce:
2 tablespoons gochujang (Korean chili paste)
1 tablespoon mayonnaise
1 tablespoon toasted sesame oil

1 tablespoon minced fresh ginger
1 tablespoon minced garlic
1 teaspoon sugar
1 teaspoon agave nectar or honey
For Serving
1 teaspoon sesame seeds
25 g chopped spring onions

1. For the wings: Season the wings with the salt and pepper and place in the air fryer basket. Set the air fryer to 200ºC for 20 minutes, turning the wings halfway through the cooking time.
2. Meanwhile, for the sauce: In a small bowl, combine the gochujang, mayonnaise, sesame oil, ginger, garlic, sugar, and agave; set aside.
3. As you near the 20-minute mark, use a meat thermometer to check the meat. When the wings reach 70ºC, transfer them to a large bowl. Pour about half the sauce on the wings; toss to coat (serve the remaining sauce as a dip).
4. Return the wings to the air fryer basket and cook for 5 minutes, until the sauce has glazed.
5. Transfer the wings to a serving platter. Sprinkle with the sesame seeds and spring onions. Serve with the reserved sauce on the side for dipping.

Spice-Rubbed Chicken Thighs

Prep time: 10 minutes | Cook time: 25 minutes | Serves 4

4 (115 g) bone-in, skin-on chicken thighs
½ teaspoon salt
½ teaspoon garlic powder

2 teaspoons chili powder
1 teaspoon paprika
1 teaspoon ground cumin
1 small lime, halved

1. Pat chicken thighs dry and sprinkle with salt, garlic powder, chili powder, paprika, and cumin.
2. Squeeze juice from ½ lime over thighs. Place thighs into ungreased air fryer basket. Adjust the temperature to 190ºC and roast for 25 minutes, turning thighs halfway through cooking. Thighs will be crispy and browned with an internal temperature of at least 76ºC when done.
3. Transfer thighs to a large serving plate and drizzle with remaining lime juice. Serve warm.

Herb-Buttermilk Chicken Breast

Prep time: 5 minutes | Cook time: 40 minutes | Serves 2

1 large bone-in, skin-on chicken breast
240 ml buttermilk
1½ teaspoons dried parsley
1½ teaspoons dried chives
¾ teaspoon kosher salt

½ teaspoon dried dill
½ teaspoon onion powder
¼ teaspoon garlic powder
¼ teaspoon dried tarragon
Cooking spray

1. Place the chicken breast in a bowl and pour over the buttermilk, turning the chicken in it to make sure it's completely covered. Let the chicken stand at room temperature for at least 20 minutes or in the refrigerator for up to 4 hours.
2. Meanwhile, in a bowl, stir together the parsley, chives, salt, dill, onion powder, garlic powder, and tarragon.
3. Preheat the air fryer to 150ºC.
4. Remove the chicken from the buttermilk, letting the excess drip off, then place the chicken skin-side up directly in the air fryer. Sprinkle the seasoning mix all over the top of the chicken breast, then let stand until the herb mix soaks into the buttermilk, at least 5 minutes.
5. Spray the top of the chicken with cooking spray. Bake for 10 minutes, then increase the temperature to 180ºC and bake until an instant-read thermometer inserted into the thickest part of the breast reads 80ºC and the chicken is deep golden brown, 30 to 35 minutes.
6. Transfer the chicken breast to a cutting board, let rest for 10 minutes, then cut the meat off the bone and cut into thick slices for serving.

Cajun-Breaded Chicken Bites

Prep time: 10 minutes | Cook time: 12 minutes | Serves 4

450 g boneless, skinless chicken breasts, cut into 1-inch cubes	30 g plain pork rinds, finely crushed
120 g heavy whipping cream	40 g unflavoured whey protein powder
½ teaspoon salt	½ teaspoon Cajun seasoning
¼ teaspoon ground black pepper	

1. Place chicken in a medium bowl and pour in cream. Stir to coat. Sprinkle with salt and pepper.
2. In a separate large bowl, combine pork rinds, protein powder, and Cajun seasoning. Remove chicken from cream, shaking off any excess, and toss in dry mix until fully coated.
3. Place bites into ungreased air fryer basket. Adjust the temperature to 200°C and air fry for 12 minutes, shaking the basket twice during cooking. Bites will be done when golden brown and have an internal temperature of at least 76°C. Serve warm.

Crispy Duck with Cherry Sauce

Prep time: 10 minutes | Cook time: 33 minutes | Serves 2 to 4

1 whole duck (2.3 kg), split in half, back and rib bones removed	1 shallot, minced
1 teaspoon olive oil	120 ml sherry
Salt and freshly ground black pepper, to taste	240 g cherry preserves
Cherry Sauce:	240 ml chicken stock
1 tablespoon butter	1 teaspoon white wine vinegar
	1 teaspoon fresh thyme leaves
	Salt and freshly ground black pepper, to taste

1. Preheat the air fryer to 200°C.
2. Trim some of the fat from the duck. Rub olive oil on the duck and season with salt and pepper. Place the duck halves in the air fryer basket, breast side up and facing the centre of the basket.
3. Air fry the duck for 20 minutes. Turn the duck over and air fry for another 6 minutes.
4. While duck is air frying, make the cherry sauce. Melt the butter in a large sauté pan. Add the shallot and sauté until it is just starting to brown, about 2 to 3 minutes. Add the sherry and deglaze the pan by scraping up any brown bits from the bottom of the pan. Simmer the liquid for a few minutes, until it has reduced by half. Add the cherry preserves, chicken stock and white wine vinegar. Whisk well to combine all the ingredients. Simmer the sauce until it thickens and coats the back of a spoon, about 5 to 7 minutes. Season with salt and pepper and stir in the fresh thyme leaves.
5. When the air fryer timer goes off, spoon some cherry sauce over the duck and continue to air fry at 200°C for 4 more minutes. Then, turn the duck halves back over so that the breast side is facing up.

Spoon more cherry sauce over the top of the duck, covering the skin completely. Air fry for 3 more minutes and then remove the duck to a plate to rest for a few minutes.
6. Serve the duck in halves, or cut each piece in half again for a smaller serving. Spoon any additional sauce over the duck or serve it on the side.

Peachy Chicken Chunks with Cherries

Prep time: 8 minutes | Cook time: 14 to 16 minutes | Serves 4

100 g peach preserves	450 g boneless chicken breasts, cut in 1½-inch chunks
1 teaspoon ground rosemary	Oil for misting or cooking spray
½ teaspoon black pepper	1 (280 g) package frozen unsweetened dark cherries, thawed and drained
½ teaspoon salt	
½ teaspoon marjoram	
1 teaspoon light olive oil	

1. In a medium bowl, mix together peach preserves, rosemary, pepper, salt, marjoram, and olive oil.
2. Stir in chicken chunks and toss to coat well with the preserve mixture.
3. Spray the air fryer basket with oil or cooking spray and lay chicken chunks in basket.
4. Air fry at 200°C for 7 minutes. Stir. Cook for 6 to 8 more minutes or until chicken juices run clear.
5. When chicken has cooked through, scatter the cherries over and cook for additional minute to heat cherries.

Chicken Drumsticks with Barbecue-Honey Sauce

Prep time: 5 minutes | Cook time: 40 minutes | Serves 5

1 tablespoon olive oil	Salt and ground black pepper, to taste
10 chicken drumsticks	240 ml barbecue sauce
Chicken seasoning or rub, to taste	85 g honey

1. Preheat the air fryer to 200°C. Grease the air fryer basket with olive oil.
2. Rub the chicken drumsticks with chicken seasoning or rub, salt and ground black pepper on a clean work surface.
3. Arrange the chicken drumsticks in a single layer in the air fryer, then air fry for 18 minutes or until lightly browned. Flip the drumsticks halfway through. You may need to work in batches to avoid overcrowding.
4. Meanwhile, combine the barbecue sauce and honey in a small bowl. Stir to mix well.
5. Remove the drumsticks from the air fryer and baste with the sauce mixture to serve.

Chipotle Drumsticks

Prep time: 15 minutes | Cook time: 20 minutes | Serves 4

1 tablespoon tomato paste
½ teaspoon chipotle powder
¼ teaspoon apple cider vinegar
¼ teaspoon garlic powder
8 chicken drumsticks
½ teaspoon salt
⅛ teaspoon ground black pepper

1. In a small bowl, combine tomato paste, chipotle powder, vinegar, and garlic powder.
2. Sprinkle drumsticks with salt and pepper, then place into a large bowl and pour in tomato paste mixture. Toss or stir to evenly coat all drumsticks in mixture.
3. Place drumsticks into ungreased air fryer basket. Adjust the temperature to 200ºC and air fry for 25 minutes, turning drumsticks halfway through cooking. Drumsticks will be dark red with an internal temperature of at least 76ºC when done. Serve warm.

Easy Turkey Tenderloin

Prep time: 20 minutes | Cook time: 30 minutes | Serves 4

Olive oil
½ teaspoon paprika
½ teaspoon garlic powder
½ teaspoon salt
½ teaspoon freshly ground black pepper
Pinch cayenne pepper
680 g turkey breast tenderloin

1. Spray the air fryer basket lightly with olive oil.
2. In a small bowl, combine the paprika, garlic powder, salt, black pepper, and cayenne pepper. Rub the mixture all over the turkey.
3. Place the turkey in the air fryer basket and lightly spray with olive oil.
4. Air fry at 190ºC for 15 minutes. Flip the turkey over and lightly spray with olive oil. Air fry until the internal temperature reaches at least 80ºC for an additional 10 to 15 minutes.
5. Let the turkey rest for 10 minutes before slicing and serving.

Chicken Rochambeau

Prep time: 15 minutes | Cook time: 20 minutes | Serves 4

1 tablespoon butter
4 chicken tenders, cut in half crosswise
Salt and pepper, to taste
30 g flour
Oil for misting
4 slices ham, ¼- to ⅜-inches thick and large enough to cover an English muffin
2 English muffins, split
Sauce:
2 tablespoons butter
25 g chopped green onions
50 g chopped mushrooms
2 tablespoons flour
240 ml chicken broth
¼ teaspoon garlic powder
1½ teaspoons Worcestershire

sauce

1. Place 1 tablespoon of butter in a baking pan and air fry at 200ºC for 2 minutes to melt.
2. Sprinkle chicken tenders with salt and pepper to taste, then roll in the flour.
3. Place chicken in baking pan, turning pieces to coat with melted butter.
4. Air fry at 200ºC for 5 minutes. Turn chicken pieces over, and spray tops lightly with olive oil. Cook 5 minutes longer or until juices run clear. The chicken will not brown.
5. While chicken is cooking, make the sauce: In a medium saucepan, melt the 2 tablespoons of butter.
6. Add onions and mushrooms and sauté until tender, about 3 minutes.
7. Stir in the flour. Gradually add broth, stirring constantly until you have a smooth gravy.
8. Add garlic powder and Worcestershire sauce and simmer on low heat until sauce thickens, about 5 minutes.
9. When chicken is cooked, remove baking pan from air fryer and set aside.
10. Place ham slices directly into air fryer basket and air fry at 200ºC for 5 minutes or until hot and beginning to sizzle a little. Remove and set aside on top of the chicken for now.
11. Place the English muffin halves in air fryer basket and air fry at 200ºC for 1 minute.
12. Open air fryer and place a ham slice on top of each English muffin half. Stack 2 pieces of chicken on top of each ham slice. Air fry for 1 to 2 minutes to heat through.
13. Place each English muffin stack on a serving plate and top with plenty of sauce.

Cranberry Curry Chicken

Prep time: 12 minutes | Cook time: 18 minutes | Serves 4

3 (140 g) low-sodium boneless, skinless chicken breasts, cut into 1½-inch cubes
2 teaspoons olive oil
2 tablespoons cornflour
1 tablespoon curry powder
1 tart apple, chopped
120 ml low-sodium chicken broth
60 g dried cranberries
2 tablespoons freshly squeezed orange juice
Brown rice, cooked (optional)

1. Preheat the air fryer to 196ºC.
2. In a medium bowl, mix the chicken and olive oil. Sprinkle with the cornflour and curry powder. Toss to coat. Stir in the apple and transfer to a metal pan. Bake in the air fryer for 8 minutes, stirring once during cooking.
3. Add the chicken broth, cranberries, and orange juice. Bake for about 10 minutes more, or until the sauce is slightly thickened and the chicken reaches an internal temperature of 76ºC on a meat thermometer. Serve over hot cooked brown rice, if desired.

Hawaiian Huli Huli Chicken

Prep time: 30 minutes | Cook time: 15 minutes | Serves 4

4 boneless, skinless chicken thighs (680 g)	50 g sugar
1 (230 g) can pineapple chunks in juice, drained, 60 ml juice reserved	2 tablespoons ketchup
60 ml soy sauce	1 tablespoon minced fresh ginger
	1 tablespoon minced garlic
	25 g chopped spring onions

1. Use a fork to pierce the chicken all over to allow the marinade to penetrate better. Place the chicken in a large bowl or large resealable plastic bag.

2. Set the drained pineapple chunks aside. In a small microwave-safe bowl, combine the pineapple juice, soy sauce, sugar, ketchup, ginger, and garlic. Pour half the sauce over the chicken; toss to coat. Reserve the remaining sauce. Marinate the chicken at room temperature for 30 minutes, or cover and refrigerate for up to 24 hours.

3. Place the chicken in the air fryer basket. (Discard marinade.) Set the air fryer to 180ºC for 15 minutes, turning halfway through the cooking time.

4. Meanwhile, microwave the reserved sauce on high for 45 to 60 seconds, stirring every 15 seconds, until the sauce has the consistency of a thick glaze.

5. At the end of the cooking time, use a meat thermometer to ensure the chicken has reached an internal temperature of 76ºC.

6. Transfer the chicken to a serving platter. Pour the sauce over the chicken. Garnish with the pineapple chunks and spring onions.

Chicken Paillard

Prep time: 10 minutes | Cook time: 10 minutes | Serves 2

2 large eggs, room temperature	Lemon Butter Sauce:
1 tablespoon water	2 tablespoons unsalted butter, melted
40 g powdered Parmesan cheese or pork dust	2 teaspoons lemon juice
2 teaspoons dried thyme leaves	¼ teaspoon finely chopped fresh thyme leaves, plus more for garnish
1 teaspoon ground black pepper	
2 (140 g) boneless, skinless chicken breasts, pounded to ½ inch thick	⅛ teaspoon fine sea salt
	Lemon slices, for serving

1. Spray the air fryer basket with avocado oil. Preheat the air fryer to 200ºC.

2. Beat the eggs in a shallow dish, then add the water and stir well.

3. In a separate shallow dish, mix together the Parmesan, thyme, and pepper until well combined.

4. One at a time, dip the chicken breasts in the eggs and let any excess drip off, then dredge both sides of the chicken in the Parmesan mixture. As you finish, set the coated chicken in the air fryer basket.

5. Roast the chicken in the air fryer for 5 minutes, then flip the chicken and cook for another 5 minutes, or until cooked through and the internal temperature reaches 76ºC.

6. While the chicken cooks, make the lemon butter sauce: In a small bowl, mix together all the sauce ingredients until well combined.

7. Plate the chicken and pour the sauce over it. Garnish with chopped fresh thyme and serve with lemon slices.

8. Store leftovers in an airtight container in the refrigerator for up to 4 days. Reheat in a preheated 200ºC air fryer for 5 minutes, or until heated through.

Turkish Chicken Kebabs

Prep time: 30 minutes | Cook time: 15 minutes | Serves 4

70 g plain Greek yogurt	1 teaspoon sweet Hungarian paprika
1 tablespoon minced garlic	
1 tablespoon tomato paste	½ teaspoon ground cinnamon
1 tablespoon fresh lemon juice	½ teaspoon black pepper
1 tablespoon vegetable oil	½ teaspoon cayenne pepper
1 teaspoon kosher salt	450 g boneless, skinless chicken thighs, quartered crosswise
1 teaspoon ground cumin	

1. In a large bowl, combine the yogurt, garlic, tomato paste, lemon juice, vegetable oil, salt, cumin, paprika, cinnamon, black pepper, and cayenne. Stir until the spices are blended into the yogurt.

2. Add the chicken to the bowl and toss until well coated. Marinate at room temperature for 30 minutes, or cover and refrigerate for up to 24 hours.

3. Arrange the chicken in a single layer in the air fryer basket. Set the air fryer to (190ºC for 10 minutes. Turn the chicken and cook for 5 minutes more. Use a meat thermometer to ensure the chicken has reached an internal temperature of 76ºC.

Chicken Nuggets

Prep time: 10 minutes | Cook time: 15 minutes | Serves 4

450 g chicken mince thighs	½ teaspoon salt
110 g shredded Mozzarella cheese	¼ teaspoon dried oregano
1 large egg, whisked	¼ teaspoon garlic powder

1. In a large bowl, combine all ingredients. Form mixture into twenty nugget shapes, about 2 tablespoons each.

2. Place nuggets into ungreased air fryer basket, working in batches if needed. Adjust the temperature to (190ºC and air fry for 15 minutes, turning nuggets halfway through cooking. Let cool 5 minutes before serving.

Chicken Pesto Pizzas

Prep time: 10 minutes | Cook time: 12 minutes | Serves 4

450 g chicken mince thighs
¼ teaspoon salt
⅛ teaspoon ground black pepper
20 g basil pesto

225 g shredded Mozzarella cheese
4 grape tomatoes, sliced

1. Cut four squares of parchment paper to fit into your air fryer basket.
2. Place chicken mince in a large bowl and mix with salt and pepper. Divide mixture into four equal sections.
3. Wet your hands with water to prevent sticking, then press each section into a 6-inch circle onto a piece of ungreased parchment. Place each chicken crust into air fryer basket, working in batches if needed.
4. Adjust the temperature to 180°C and air fry for 10 minutes, turning crusts halfway through cooking.
5. Spread 1 tablespoon pesto across the top of each crust, then sprinkle with ¼ of the Mozzarella and top with 1 sliced tomato. Continue cooking at 180°C for 2 minutes. Cheese will be melted and brown when done. Serve warm.

Israeli Chicken Schnitzel

Prep time: 5 minutes | Cook time: 10 minutes | Serves 4

2 large boneless, skinless chicken breasts, each weighing about 450 g
125 g all-purpose flour
2 teaspoons garlic powder
2 teaspoons kosher salt

1 teaspoon black pepper
1 teaspoon paprika
2 eggs beaten with 2 tablespoons water
250 g panko bread crumbs
Vegetable oil spray
Lemon juice, for serving

1. Preheat the air fryer to 190°C.
2. Place 1 chicken breast between 2 pieces of plastic wrap. Use a mallet or a rolling pin to pound the chicken until it is ¼ inch thick. Set aside. Repeat with the second breast. Whisk together the flour, garlic powder, salt, pepper, and paprika on a large plate. Place the panko in a separate shallow bowl or pie plate.
3. Dredge 1 chicken breast in the flour, shaking off any excess, then dip it in the egg mixture. Dredge the chicken breast in the panko, making sure to coat it completely. Shake off any excess panko. Place the battered chicken breast on a plate. Repeat with the second chicken breast.
4. Spray the air fryer basket with oil spray. Place 1 of the battered chicken breasts in the basket and spray the top with oil spray. Air fry until the top is browned, about 5 minutes. Flip the chicken and spray the second side with oil spray. Air fry until the second side is browned and crispy and the internal temperature reaches 76°C. Remove the first chicken breast from the air fryer and repeat with the second chicken breast.
5. Serve hot with lemon juice.

Porchetta-Style Chicken Breasts

Prep time: 10 minutes | Cook time: 15 minutes | Serves 4

25 g fresh parsley leaves
10 g roughly chopped fresh chives
4 cloves garlic, peeled
2 tablespoons lemon juice
3 teaspoons fine sea salt
1 teaspoon dried rubbed sage
1 teaspoon fresh rosemary

leaves
1 teaspoon ground fennel
½ teaspoon red pepper flakes
4 (115 g) boneless, skinless chicken breasts, pounded to ¼ inch thick
8 slices bacon
Sprigs of fresh rosemary, for garnish (optional)

1. Spray the air fryer basket with avocado oil. Preheat the air fryer to 170°C.
2. Place the parsley, chives, garlic, lemon juice, salt, sage, rosemary, fennel, and red pepper flakes in a food processor and purée until a smooth paste forms.
3. Place the chicken breasts on a cutting board and rub the paste all over the tops. With a short end facing you, roll each breast up like a jelly roll to make a log and secure it with toothpicks.
4. Wrap 2 slices of bacon around each chicken breast log to cover the entire breast. Secure the bacon with toothpicks.
5. Place the chicken breast logs in the air fryer basket and air fry for 5 minutes, flip the logs over, and cook for another 5 minutes. Increase the heat to 200°C and cook until the bacon is crisp, about 5 minutes more.
6. Remove the toothpicks and garnish with fresh rosemary sprigs, if desired, before serving. Store leftovers in an airtight container in the refrigerator for up to 4 days or in the freezer for up to a month. Reheat in a preheated 180°C air fryer for 5 minutes, then increase the heat to 200°C and cook for 2 minutes to crisp the bacon.

Italian Chicken Thighs

Prep time: 5 minutes | Cook time: 20 minutes | Serves 2

4 bone-in, skin-on chicken thighs
2 tablespoons unsalted butter, melted

1 teaspoon dried parsley
1 teaspoon dried basil
½ teaspoon garlic powder
¼ teaspoon onion powder
¼ teaspoon dried oregano

1. Brush chicken thighs with butter and sprinkle remaining ingredients over thighs. Place thighs into the air fryer basket.
2. Adjust the temperature to 190°C and roast for 20 minutes.
3. Halfway through the cooking time, flip the thighs.
4. When fully cooked, internal temperature will be at least 76°C and skin will be crispy. Serve warm.

Chicken and Gruyère Cordon Bleu

Prep time: 15 minutes | Cook time: 15 minutes | Serves 4

4 chicken breast filets
75 g chopped ham
75 g grated Swiss cheese, or Gruyère cheese
30 g all-purpose flour
Pinch salt

Freshly ground black pepper, to taste
½ teaspoon dried marjoram
1 egg
120 g panko bread crumbs
Olive oil spray

1. Put the chicken breast filets on a work surface and gently press them with the palm of your hand to make them a bit thinner. Don't tear the meat.

2. In a small bowl, combine the ham and cheese. Divide this mixture among the chicken filets. Wrap the chicken around the filling to enclose it, using toothpicks to hold the chicken together.

3. In a shallow bowl, stir together the flour, salt, pepper, and marjoram.

4. In another bowl, beat the egg.

5. Spread the panko on a plate.

6. Dip the chicken in the flour mixture, in the egg, and in the panko to coat thoroughly. Press the crumbs into the chicken so they stick well.

7. Insert the crisper plate into the basket and the basket into the unit. Preheat the unit by selecting BAKE, setting the temperature to 190ºC, and setting the time to 3 minutes. Select START/STOP to begin.

8. Once the unit is preheated, spray the crisper plate with olive oil. Place the chicken into the basket and spray it with olive oil.

9. Select BAKE, set the temperature to 190ºC, and set the time to 15 minutes. Select START/STOP to begin.

10. When the cooking is complete, the chicken should be cooked through and a food thermometer inserted into the chicken should register 76ºC. Carefully remove the toothpicks and serve.

Chapter 4 Snacks and Appetisers

Red Pepper Tapenade

Prep time: 5 minutes | Cook time: 5 minutes | Serves 4

1 large red pepper
2 tablespoons plus 1 teaspoon olive oil, divided
120 ml Kalamata olives, pitted
and roughly chopped
1 garlic clove, minced
½ teaspoon dried oregano
1 tablespoon lemon juice

1. Preheat the air fryer to 192°C.
2. Brush the outside of a whole red pepper with 1 teaspoon olive oil and place it inside the air fryer basket. Roast for 5 minutes.
3. Meanwhile, in a medium bowl combine the remaining 2 tablespoons of olive oil with the olives, garlic, oregano, and lemon juice.
4. Remove the red pepper from the air fryer, then gently slice off the stem and remove the seeds. Roughly chop the roasted pepper into small pieces.
5. Add the red pepper to the olive mixture and stir all together until combined.
6. Serve with pitta chips, crackers, or crusty bread.

Cheesy Courgette Tots

Prep time: 15 minutes | Cook time: 6 minutes | Serves 8

2 medium courgette (about 340 g), shredded
1 large egg, whisked
120 ml grated pecorino Romano cheese
120 ml panko breadcrumbs
¼ teaspoon black pepper
1 clove garlic, minced
Cooking spray

1. Using your hands, squeeze out as much liquid from the courgette as possible. In a large bowl, mix the courgette with the remaining ingredients except the oil until well incorporated.
2. Make the courgette tots: Use a spoon or cookie scoop to place tablespoonfuls of the courgette mixture onto a lightly floured cutting board and form into 1-inch logs.
3. Preheat air fryer to 192°C. Spritz the air fryer basket with cooking spray.
4. Place the tots in the basket. You may need to cook in batches to avoid overcrowding.
5. Air fry for 6 minutes until golden brown.
6. Remove from the basket to a serving plate and repeat with the remaining courgette tots.
7. Serve immediately.

Sea Salt Potato Crisps

Prep time: 30 minutes | Cook time: 27 minutes | Serves 4

Oil, for spraying
4 medium yellow potatoes such as Maris Pipers
1 tablespoon oil
⅛ to ¼ teaspoon fine sea salt

1. Line the air fryer basket with parchment and spray lightly with oil.
2. Using a mandoline or a very sharp knife, cut the potatoes into very thin slices.
3. Place the slices in a bowl of cold water and let soak for about 20 minutes.
4. Drain the potatoes, transfer them to a plate lined with paper towels, and pat dry.
5. Drizzle the oil over the potatoes, sprinkle with the salt, and toss to combine. Transfer to the prepared basket.
6. Air fry at 92°C for 20 minutes. Toss the crisps, increase the heat to 204°C, and cook for another 5 to 7 minutes, until crispy.

Cinnamon-Apple Crisps

Prep time: 10 minutes | Cook time: 32 minutes | Serves 4

Oil, for spraying
2 Red Delicious or Honeycrisp apples
¼ teaspoon ground cinnamon, divided

1. Line the air fryer basket with parchment and spray lightly with oil.
2. Trim the uneven ends off the apples. Using a mandoline slicer on the thinnest setting or a sharp knife, cut the apples into very thin slices. Discard the cores.
3. Place half of the apple slices in a single layer in the prepared basket and sprinkle with half of the cinnamon.
4. Place a metal air fryer trivet on top of the apples to keep them from flying around while they are cooking.
5. Air fry at 148°C for 16 minutes, flipping every 5 minutes to ensure even cooking. Repeat with the remaining apple slices and cinnamon.
6. Let cool to room temperature before serving. The crisps will firm up as they cool.

Garlic-Parmesan Croutons

Prep time: 3 minutes | Cook time: 12 minutes | Serves 4

Oil, for spraying
1 L cubed French bread
1 tablespoon grated Parmesan cheese
3 tablespoons olive oil
1 tablespoon granulated garlic
½ teaspoon unsalted salt

1. Line the air fryer basket with parchment and spray lightly with oil.
2. In a large bowl, mix together the bread, Parmesan cheese, olive oil, garlic, and salt, tossing with your hands to evenly distribute the seasonings. Transfer the coated bread cubes to the prepared basket.
3. Air fry at 176ºC for 10 to 12 minutes, stirring once after 5 minutes, or until crisp and golden brown.

Artichoke and Olive Pitta Flatbread

Prep time: 5 minutes | Cook time: 10 minutes | Serves 4

2 wholewheat pittas
2 tablespoons olive oil, divided
2 garlic cloves, minced
¼ teaspoon salt
120 ml canned artichoke hearts, sliced
60 ml Kalamata olives
60 ml shredded Parmesan
60 ml crumbled feta
Chopped fresh parsley, for garnish (optional)

1. Preheat the air fryer to 192ºC.
2. Brush each pitta with 1 tablespoon olive oil, then sprinkle the minced garlic and salt over the top.
3. Distribute the artichoke hearts, olives, and cheeses evenly between the two pittas, and place both into the air fryer to bake for 10 minutes.
4. Remove the pittas and cut them into 4 pieces each before serving. Sprinkle parsley over the top, if desired.

Bacon-Wrapped Pickle Spears

Prep time: 10 minutes | Cook time: 8 minutes | Serves 4

8 to 12 slices bacon
60 ml soft white cheese
60 ml shredded Mozzarella
cheese
8 dill pickle spears
120 ml ranch dressing

1. Lay the bacon slices on a flat surface. In a medium bowl, combine the soft white cheese and Mozzarella. Stir until well blended. Spread the cheese mixture over the bacon slices.
2. Place a pickle spear on a bacon slice and roll the bacon around the pickle in a spiral, ensuring the pickle is fully covered. (You may need to use more than one slice of bacon per pickle to fully cover the spear.) Tuck in the ends to ensure the bacon stays put. Repeat to wrap all the pickles.
3. Place the wrapped pickles in the air fryer basket in a single layer. Set the air fryer to 204ºC for 8 minutes, or until the bacon is cooked through and crisp on the edges.
4. Serve the pickle spears with ranch dressing on the side.

Lebanese Muhammara

Prep time: 15 minutes | Cook time: 15 minutes | Serves 6

2 large red peppers
60 ml plus 2 tablespoons extra-virgin olive oil
240 ml walnut halves
1 tablespoon agave nectar or honey
1 teaspoon fresh lemon juice
1 teaspoon ground cumin
1 teaspoon rock salt
1 teaspoon red pepper flakes
Raw vegetables (such as cucumber, carrots, courgette slices, or cauliflower) or toasted pitta chips, for serving

1. Drizzle the peppers with 2 tablespoons of the olive oil and place in the air fryer basket. Set the air fryer to 204ºC for 10 minutes.
2. Add the walnuts to the basket, arranging them around the peppers. Set the air fryer to 204ºC for 5 minutes.
3. Remove the peppers, seal in a resealable plastic bag, and let rest for 5 to 10 minutes. Transfer the walnuts to a plate and set aside to cool.
4. Place the softened peppers, walnuts, agave, lemon juice, cumin, salt, and ½ teaspoon of the pepper flakes in a food processor and purée until smooth.
5. Transfer the dip to a serving bowl and make an indentation in the middle. Pour the remaining 60 ml olive oil into the indentation. Garnish the dip with the remaining ½ teaspoon pepper flakes.
6. Serve with vegetables or toasted pitta chips.

Roasted Grape Dip

Prep time: 10 minutes | Cook time: 8 to 12 minutes | Serves 6

475 ml seedless red grapes, rinsed and patted dry
1 tablespoon apple cider vinegar
1 tablespoon honey
240 ml low-fat Greek yoghurt
2 tablespoons semi-skimmed milk
2 tablespoons minced fresh basil

1. In the air fryer basket, sprinkle the grapes with the cider vinegar and drizzle with the honey. Toss to coat. Roast the grapes at 192ºC for 8 to 12 minutes, or until shrivelled but still soft. Remove from the air fryer.
2. In a medium bowl, stir together the yoghurt and milk.
3. Gently blend in the grapes and basil. Serve immediately or cover and chill for 1 to 2 hours.

Veggie Salmon Nachos

Prep time: 10 minutes | Cook time: 9 to 12 minutes | Serves 6

57 g baked no-salt corn tortilla chips
1 (142 g) baked salmon fillet, flaked
120 ml canned low-salt black beans, rinsed and drained
1 red pepper, chopped
120 ml grated carrot
1 jalapeño pepper, minced
80 ml shredded low-salt low-fat Swiss cheese
1 tomato, chopped

1. Preheat the air fryer to 182°C.
2. In a baking pan, layer the tortilla chips. Top with the salmon, black beans, red pepper, carrot, jalapeño, and Swiss cheese.
3. Bake in the air fryer for 9 to 12 minutes, or until the cheese is melted and starts to brown.
4. Top with the tomato and serve.

Air Fried Pot Stickers

Prep time: 10 minutes | Cook time: 18 to 20 minutes | Makes 30 pot stickers

120 ml finely chopped cabbage
60 ml finely chopped red pepper
2 spring onions, finely chopped
1 egg, beaten
2 tablespoons cocktail sauce
2 teaspoons low-salt soy sauce
30 wonton wrappers
1 tablespoon water, for brushing the wrappers

1. Preheat the air fryer to 182°C.
2. In a small bowl, combine the cabbage, pepper, spring onions, egg, cocktail sauce, and soy sauce, and mix well.
3. Put about 1 teaspoon of the mixture in the centre of each wonton wrapper. Fold the wrapper in half, covering the filling; dampen the edges with water, and seal. You can crimp the edges of the wrapper with your fingers, so they look like the pot stickers you get in restaurants. Brush them with water.
4. Place the pot stickers in the air fryer basket and air fry in 2 batches for 9 to 10 minutes, or until the pot stickers are hot and the bottoms are lightly browned.
5. Serve hot.

Courgette Fries with Roasted Garlic Aioli

Prep time: 20 minutes | Cook time: 12 minutes | Serves 4

1 tablespoon vegetable oil
½ head green or savoy cabbage, finely shredded
Roasted Garlic Aioli:
1 teaspoon roasted garlic
120 ml mayonnaise
2 tablespoons olive oil
Juice of ½ lemon
Salt and pepper, to taste
Courgette Fries:

120 ml flour
2 eggs, beaten
240 ml seasoned breadcrumbs
Salt and pepper, to taste
1 large courgette, cut into ½-inch sticks
Olive oil

1. Make the aioli: Combine the roasted garlic, mayonnaise, olive oil and lemon juice in a bowl and whisk well. Season the aioli with salt and pepper to taste.
2. Prepare the courgette fries. Create a dredging station with three shallow dishes. Place the flour in the first shallow dish and season well with salt and freshly ground black pepper. Put the beaten eggs in the second shallow dish. In the third shallow dish, combine the breadcrumbs, salt and pepper. Dredge the courgette sticks, coating with flour first, then dipping them into the eggs to coat, and finally tossing in breadcrumbs. Shake the dish with the breadcrumbs and pat the crumbs onto the courgette sticks gently with your hands, so they stick evenly.
3. Place the courgette fries on a flat surface and let them sit at least 10 minutes before air frying to let them dry out a little. Preheat the air fryer to 204°C.
4. Spray the courgette sticks with olive oil and place them into the air fryer basket. You can air fry the courgette in two layers, placing the second layer in the opposite direction to the first. Air fry for 12 minutes turning and rotating the fries halfway through the cooking time. Spray with additional oil when you turn them over.
5. Serve courgette fries warm with the roasted garlic aioli.

Rosemary-Garlic Shoestring Fries

Prep time: 5 minutes | Cook time: 18 minutes | Serves 2

1 large russet or Maris Piper potato (about 340 g), scrubbed clean, and julienned
1 tablespoon vegetable oil
Leaves from 1 sprig fresh
rosemary
Rock salt and freshly ground black pepper, to taste
1 garlic clove, thinly sliced
Flaky sea salt, for serving

1. Preheat the air fryer to 204°C.
2. Place the julienned potatoes in a large colander and rinse under cold running water until the water runs clear. Spread the potatoes out on a double-thick layer of paper towels and pat dry.
3. In a large bowl, combine the potatoes, oil, and rosemary. Season with rock salt and pepper and toss to coat evenly. Place the potatoes in the air fryer and air fry for 18 minutes, shaking the basket every 5 minutes and adding the garlic in the last 5 minutes of cooking, or until the fries are golden brown and crisp.
4. Transfer the fries to a plate and sprinkle with flaky sea salt while they're hot. Serve immediately.

Spiralized Potato Nest with Tomato Ketchup

Prep time: 10 minutes | Cook time: 15 minutes | Serves 2

1 large russet or Maris Piper potato (about 340 g)	120 ml canned crushed tomatoes
2 tablespoons vegetable oil	2 tablespoons apple cider vinegar
1 tablespoon hot smoked paprika	1 tablespoon dark brown sugar
½ teaspoon garlic powder	1 tablespoon Worcestershire sauce
Rock salt and freshly ground black pepper, to taste	1 teaspoon mild hot sauce

1. Using a spiralizer, spiralize the potato, then place in a large colander. (If you don't have a spiralizer, cut the potato into thin ⅛-inch-thick matchsticks.) Rinse the potatoes under cold running water until the water runs clear. Spread the potatoes out on a double-thick layer of paper towels and pat completely dry.
2. In a large bowl, combine the potatoes, oil, paprika, and garlic powder. Season with salt and pepper and toss to combine. Transfer the potatoes to the air fryer and air fry at 204°C until the potatoes are browned and crisp, 15 minutes, shaking the basket halfway through.
3. Meanwhile, in a small blender, purée the tomatoes, vinegar, brown sugar, Worcestershire, and hot sauce until smooth. Pour into a small saucepan or skillet and simmer over medium heat until reduced by half, 3 to 5 minutes. Pour the homemade ketchup into a bowl and let cool.
4. Remove the spiralized potato nest from the air fryer and serve hot with the ketchup.

Shrimp Pirogues

Prep time: 15 minutes | Cook time: 4 to 5 minutes | Serves 8

340 g small, peeled, and deveined raw shrimp	1 teaspoon dried dill weed, crushed
85 g soft white cheese, room temperature	Salt, to taste
2 tablespoons natural yoghurt	4 small hothouse cucumbers, each approximately 6 inches long
1 teaspoon lemon juice	

1. Pour 4 tablespoons water in bottom of air fryer drawer.
2. Place shrimp in air fryer basket in single layer and air fry at 200°C for 4 to 5 minutes, just until done. Watch carefully because shrimp cooks quickly, and overcooking makes it tough.
3. Chop shrimp into small pieces, no larger than ½ inch. Refrigerate while mixing the remaining ingredients.
4. With a fork, mash and whip the soft white cheese until smooth.
5. Stir in the yoghurt and beat until smooth. Stir in lemon juice, dill weed, and chopped shrimp.
6. Taste for seasoning. If needed, add ¼ to ½ teaspoon salt to suit your taste.
7. Store in refrigerator until serving time.
8. When ready to serve, wash and dry cucumbers and split them lengthwise. Scoop out the seeds and turn cucumbers upside down on paper towels to drain for 10 minutes.
9. Just before filling, wipe centres of cucumbers dry. Spoon the shrimp mixture into the pirogues and cut in half crosswise. Serve immediately.

Fried Artichoke Hearts

Prep time: 10 minutes | Cook time: 12 minutes | Serves 10

Oil, for spraying	240 ml panko breadcrumbs
3 (397 g) cans quartered artichokes, drained and patted dry	80 ml grated Parmesan cheese
120 ml mayonnaise	Salt and freshly ground black pepper, to taste

1. Line the air fryer basket with parchment and spray lightly with oil.
2. Place the artichokes on a plate. Put the mayonnaise and breadcrumbs in separate bowls.
3. Working one at a time, dredge each artichoke piece in the mayonnaise, then in the breadcrumbs to cover.
4. Place the artichokes in the prepared basket. You may need to work in batches, depending on the size of your air fryer.
5. Air fry at 188°C for 10 to 12 minutes, or until crispy and golden brown.
6. Sprinkle with the Parmesan cheese and season with salt and black pepper. Serve immediately.

Black Bean Corn Dip

Prep time: 10 minutes | Cook time: 10 minutes | Serves 4

½ (425 g) can black beans, drained and rinsed	60 ml shredded low-fat Cheddar cheese
½ (425 g) can corn, drained and rinsed	½ teaspoon ground cumin
60 ml chunky salsa	½ teaspoon paprika
57 g low-fat soft white cheese	Salt and freshly ground black pepper, to taste

1. Preheat the air fryer to 164°C.
2. In a medium bowl, mix together the black beans, corn, salsa, soft white cheese, Cheddar cheese, cumin, and paprika. Season with salt and pepper and stir until well combined.
3. Spoon the mixture into a baking dish.
4. Place baking dish in the air fryer basket and bake until heated through, about 10 minutes.
5. Serve hot.

Polenta Fries with Chilli-Lime Mayo

Prep time: 10 minutes | Cook time: 28 minutes | Serves 4

Polenta Fries:
2 teaspoons vegetable or olive oil
¼ teaspoon paprika
450 g prepared polenta, cut into 3-inch × ½-inch strips
Chilli-Lime Mayo:
120 ml mayonnaise

1 teaspoon chilli powder
1 teaspoon chopped fresh coriander
¼ teaspoon ground cumin
Juice of ½ lime
Salt and freshly ground black pepper, to taste

1. Preheat the air fryer to 204ºC.
2. Mix the oil and paprika in a bowl. Add the polenta strips and toss until evenly coated.
3. Transfer the polenta strips to the air fry basket and air fry for 28 minutes until the fries are golden brown, shaking the basket once during cooking. Season as desired with salt and pepper.
4. Meanwhile, whisk together all the ingredients for the chilli-lime mayo in a small bowl.
5. Remove the polenta fries from the air fryer to a plate and serve alongside the chilli-lime mayo as a dipping sauce.

Pepperoni Pizza Dip

Prep time: 10 minutes | Cook time: 10 minutes | Serves 6

170 g soft white cheese
177 ml shredded Italian cheese blend
60 ml sour cream
1½ teaspoons dried Italian seasoning
¼ teaspoon garlic salt
¼ teaspoon onion powder
177 ml pizza sauce

120 ml sliced miniature pepperoni
60 ml sliced black olives
1 tablespoon thinly sliced green onion
Cut-up raw vegetables, toasted baguette slices, pitta chips, or tortilla chips, for serving

1. In a small bowl, combine the soft white cheese, 60 ml of the shredded cheese, the sour cream, Italian seasoning, garlic salt, and onion powder. Stir until smooth and the ingredients are well blended.
2. Spread the mixture in a baking pan. Top with the pizza sauce, spreading to the edges. Sprinkle with the remaining 120 ml shredded cheese. Arrange the pepperoni slices on top of the cheese. Top with the black olives and green onion.
3. Place the pan in the air fryer basket. Set the air fryer to 176ºC for 10 minutes, or until the pepperoni is beginning to brown on the edges and the cheese is bubbly and lightly browned.
4. Let stand for 5 minutes before serving with vegetables, toasted baguette slices, pitta chips, or tortilla chips.

Spiced Roasted Cashews

Prep time: 5 minutes | Cook time: 10 minutes | Serves 4

475 ml raw cashews
2 tablespoons olive oil
¼ teaspoon salt

¼ teaspoon chilli powder
⅛ teaspoon garlic powder
⅛ teaspoon smoked paprika

1. Preheat the air fryer to 182ºC.
2. In a large bowl, toss all of the ingredients together.
3. Pour the cashews into the air fryer basket and roast them for 5 minutes. Shake the basket, then cook for 5 minutes more.
4. Serve immediately.

Kale Chips with Sesame

Prep time: 15 minutes | Cook time: 8 minutes | Serves 5

2 L deribbed kale leaves, torn into 2-inch pieces
1½ tablespoons olive oil
¾ teaspoon chilli powder

¼ teaspoon garlic powder
½ teaspoon paprika
2 teaspoons sesame seeds

1. Preheat air fryer to 176ºC.
2. In a large bowl, toss the kale with the olive oil, chilli powder, garlic powder, paprika, and sesame seeds until well coated.
3. Put the kale in the air fryer basket and air fry for 8 minutes, flipping the kale twice during cooking, or until the kale is crispy.
4. Serve warm.

Easy Spiced Nuts

Prep time: 5 minutes | Cook time: 25 minutes | Makes 3 L

1 egg white, lightly beaten
60 ml sugar
1 teaspoon salt
½ teaspoon ground cinnamon
¼ teaspoon ground cloves

¼ teaspoon ground allspice
Pinch ground cayenne pepper
240 ml pecan halves
240 ml cashews
240 ml almonds

1. Combine the egg white with the sugar and spices in a bowl.
2. Preheat the air fryer to 148ºC.
3. Spray or brush the air fryer basket with vegetable oil. Toss the nuts together in the spiced egg white and transfer the nuts to the air fryer basket.
4. Air fry for 25 minutes, stirring the nuts in the basket a few times during the cooking process. Taste the nuts (carefully because they will be very hot) to see if they are crunchy and nicely toasted. Air fry for a few more minutes if necessary.
5. Serve warm or cool to room temperature and store in an airtight container for up to two weeks.

Dark Chocolate and Cranberry Granola Bars

Prep time: 5 minutes | Cook time: 15 minutes | Serves 6

475 ml certified gluten-free quick oats	3 tablespoons unsweetened shredded coconut
2 tablespoons sugar-free dark chocolate chunks	120 ml raw honey
2 tablespoons unsweetened dried cranberries	1 teaspoon ground cinnamon
	⅛ teaspoon salt
	2 tablespoons olive oil

1. Preheat the air fryer to 182ºC. Line an 8-by-8-inch baking dish with parchment paper that comes up the side so you can lift it out after cooking.
2. In a large bowl, mix together all of the ingredients until well combined.
3. Press the oat mixture into the pan in an even layer.
4. Place the pan into the air fryer basket and bake for 15 minutes.
5. Remove the pan from the air fryer and lift the granola cake out of the pan using the edges of the parchment paper.
6. Allow to cool for 5 minutes before slicing into 6 equal bars.
7. Serve immediately or wrap in plastic wrap and store at room temperature for up to 1 week.

Spinach and Crab Meat Cups

Prep time: 10 minutes | Cook time: 10 minutes | Makes 30 cups

1 (170 g) can crab meat, drained to yield 80 ml meat	¼ teaspoon lemon juice
60 ml frozen spinach, thawed, drained, and chopped	½ teaspoon Worcestershire sauce
1 clove garlic, minced	30 mini frozen filo shells, thawed
120 ml grated Parmesan cheese	Cooking spray
3 tablespoons plain yoghurt	

1. Preheat the air fryer to 200ºC.
2. Remove any bits of shell that might remain in the crab meat.
3. Mix the crab meat, spinach, garlic, and cheese together.
4. Stir in the yoghurt, lemon juice, and Worcestershire sauce and mix well.
5. Spoon a teaspoon of filling into each filo shell.
6. Spray the air fryer basket with cooking spray and arrange half the shells in the basket. Air fry for 5 minutes. Repeat with the remaining shells.
7. Serve immediately.

Root Veggie Chips with Herb Salt

Prep time: 10 minutes | Cook time: 8 minutes | Serves 2

1 parsnip, washed	Cooking spray
1 small beetroot, washed	Herb Salt:
1 small turnip, washed	¼ teaspoon rock salt
½ small sweet potato, washed	2 teaspoons finely chopped
1 teaspoon olive oil	fresh parsley

1. Preheat the air fryer to 182ºC.
2. Peel and thinly slice the parsnip, beetroot, turnip, and sweet potato, then place the vegetables in a large bowl, add the olive oil, and toss.
3. Spray the air fryer basket with cooking spray, then place the vegetables in the basket and air fry for 8 minutes, gently shaking the basket halfway through.
4. While the chips cook, make the herb salt in a small bowl by combining the rock salt and parsley.
5. Remove the chips and place on a serving plate, then sprinkle the herb salt on top and allow to cool for 2 to 3 minutes before serving.

Chapter 5 Fish and Seafood

Chapter 5 Fish and Seafood

Fried Prawns

Prep time: 15 minutes | Cook time: 5 minutes | Serves 4

70 g self-raising flour
1 teaspoon paprika
1 teaspoon salt
½ teaspoon freshly ground black pepper
1 large egg, beaten

120 g finely crushed panko bread crumbs
20 frozen large prawns (about 900 g), peeled and deveined
Cooking spray

1. In a shallow bowl, whisk the flour, paprika, salt, and pepper until blended. Add the beaten egg to a second shallow bowl and the bread crumbs to a third.
2. One at a time, dip the prawns into the flour, the egg, and the bread crumbs, coating thoroughly.
3. Preheat the air fryer to 204°C. Line the air fryer basket with baking paper.
4. Place the prawns on the baking paper and spritz with oil.
5. Air fry for 2 minutes. Shake the basket, spritz the prawns with oil, and air fry for 3 minutes more until lightly browned and crispy. Serve hot.

Country Prawns

Prep time: 10 minutes | Cook time: 15 to 20 minutes | Serves 4

455 g large prawns, peeled and deveined, with tails on
455 g smoked sausage, cut into thick slices
2 corn cobs, quartered
1 courgette, cut into bite-sized

pieces
1 red bell pepper, cut into chunks
1 tablespoon Old Bay seasoning
2 tablespoons olive oil
Cooking spray

1. Preheat the air fryer to 204°C. Spray the air fryer basket lightly with cooking spray.
2. In a large bowl, mix the prawns, sausage, corn, courgette, bell pepper, and Old Bay seasoning, and toss to coat with the spices. Add the olive oil and toss again until evenly coated.
3. Spread the mixture in the air fryer basket in a single layer. You will need to cook in batches.
4. Air fry for 15 to 20 minutes, or until cooked through, shaking the basket every 5 minutes for even cooking.
5. Serve immediately.

Orange-Mustard Glazed Salmon

Prep time: 10 minutes | Cook time: 10 minutes | Serves 2

1 tablespoon orange marmalade
¼ teaspoon grated orange zest plus 1 tablespoon juice
2 teaspoons whole-grain mustard

2 (230 g) skin-on salmon fillets, 1½ inches thick
Salt and pepper, to taste
Vegetable oil spray

1. Preheat the air fryer to 204°C.
2. Make foil sling for air fryer basket by folding 1 long sheet of aluminum foil so it is 4 inches wide. Lay sheet of foil widthwise across basket, pressing foil into and up sides of basket. Fold excess foil as needed so that edges of foil are flush with top of basket. Lightly spray foil and basket with vegetable oil spray.
3. Combine marmalade, orange zest and juice, and mustard in bowl. Pat salmon dry with paper towels and season with salt and pepper. Brush tops and sides of fillets evenly with glaze. Arrange fillets skin side down on sling in prepared basket, spaced evenly apart. Air fry salmon until center is still translucent when checked with the tip of a paring knife and registers 52°C (for medium-rare), 10 to 14 minutes, using sling to rotate fillets halfway through cooking.
4. Using the sling, carefully remove salmon from air fryer. Slide fish spatula along underside of fillets and transfer to individual serving plates, leaving skin behind. Serve.

Quick Prawns Skewers

Prep time: 10 minutes | Cook time: 5 minutes | Serves 5

1.8kg prawns, peeled and deveined
1 tablespoon dried rosemary

1 tablespoon avocado oil
1 teaspoon apple cider vinegar

1. Mix the prawns with dried rosemary, avocado oil, and apple cider vinegar.
2. Then thread the prawns onto skewers and put in the air fryer.
3. Cook the prawns at 204°C for 5 minutes.

Fish Fillets with Lemon-Dill Sauce

Prep time: 5 minutes | Cook time: 7 minutes | Serves 4

455 g snapper, grouper, or salmon fillets
Sea salt and freshly ground black pepper, to taste
1 tablespoon avocado oil
60 g sour cream

60 g mayonnaise
2 tablespoons fresh dill, chopped, plus more for garnish
1 tablespoon freshly squeezed lemon juice
½ teaspoon grated lemon zest

1. Pat the fish dry with paper towels and season well with salt and pepper. Brush with the avocado oil.
2. Set the air fryer to 204ºC. Place the fillets in the air fryer basket and air fry for 1 minute.
3. Lower the air fryer temperature to 164ºC and continue cooking for 5 minutes. Flip the fish and cook for 1 minute more or until an instant-read thermometer reads 64ºC. (If using salmon, cook it to 52ºC /125ºF for medium-rare.)
4. While the fish is cooking, make the sauce by combining the sour cream, mayonnaise, dill, lemon juice, and lemon zest in a medium bowl. Season with salt and pepper and stir until combined. Refrigerate until ready to serve.
5. Serve the fish with the sauce, garnished with the remaining dill.

Breaded Prawns Tacos

Prep time: 10 minutes | Cook time: 9 minutes | Makes 8 tacos

2 large eggs
1 teaspoon prepared yellow mustard
455 g small prawns, peeled, deveined, and tails removed
45 g finely shredded Gouda or Parmesan cheese
80 g pork scratchings ground to

dust
For Serving:
8 large round lettuce leaves
60 ml pico de gallo
20 g shredded purple cabbage
1 lemon, sliced
Guacamole (optional)

1. Preheat the air fryer to 204ºC.
2. Crack the eggs into a large bowl, add the mustard, and whisk until well combined. Add the prawns and stir well to coat.
3. In a medium-sized bowl, mix together the cheese and pork scratching dust until well combined.
4. One at a time, roll the coated prawns in the pork scratching dust mixture and use your hands to press it onto each prawns. Spray the coated prawns with avocado oil and place them in the air fryer basket, leaving space between them.
5. Air fry the prawns for 9 minutes, or until cooked through and no longer translucent, flipping after 4 minutes.
6. To serve, place a lettuce leaf on a serving plate, place several prawns on top, and top with 1½ teaspoons each of pico de gallo and purple cabbage. Squeeze some lemon juice on top and serve with guacamole, if desired.
7. Store leftover prawns in an airtight container in the refrigerator for up to 3 days. Reheat in a preheated 204ºC air fryer for 5 minutes, or until warmed through.

Crispy Herbed Salmon

Prep time: 5 minutes | Cook time: 9 to 12 minutes | Serves 4

4 skinless salmon fillets, 170 g each
3 tablespoons honey mustard
½ teaspoon dried thyme

½ teaspoon dried basil
15 g panko bread crumbs
30 g crushed ready salted crisps
2 tablespoons olive oil

1. Place the salmon on a plate. In a small bowl, combine the mustard, thyme, and basil, and spread evenly over the salmon.
2. In another small bowl, combine the bread crumbs and crisps and mix well. Drizzle in the olive oil and mix until combined.
3. Place the salmon in the air fryer basket and gently but firmly press the bread crumb mixture onto the top of each fillet.
4. Bake at 160ºC for 9 to 12 minutes or until the salmon reaches at least 64ºC on a meat thermometer and the topping is browned and crisp.

Scallops with Asparagus and Peas

Prep time: 10 minutes | Cook time: 7 to 10 minutes | Serves 4

Cooking oil spray
455 g asparagus, ends trimmed, cut into 2-inch pieces
100 g sugar snap peas
455 g sea scallops
1 tablespoon freshly squeezed

lemon juice
2 teaspoons extra-virgin olive oil
½ teaspoon dried thyme
Salt and freshly ground black pepper, to taste

1. Insert the crisper plate into the basket and the basket into the unit. Preheat the unit to 204ºC.
2. Once the unit is preheated, spray the crisper plate with cooking oil. Place the asparagus and sugar snap peas into the basket.
3. Cook for 10 minutes.
4. Meanwhile, check the scallops for a small muscle attached to the side. Pull it off and discard. In a medium bowl, toss together the scallops, lemon juice, olive oil, and thyme. Season with salt and pepper.
5. After 3 minutes, the vegetables should be just starting to get tender. Place the scallops on top of the vegetables. Reinsert the basket to resume cooking. After 3 minutes more, remove the basket and shake it. Again reinsert the basket to resume cooking.
6. When the cooking is complete, the scallops should be firm when tested with your finger and opaque in the center, and the vegetables tender. Serve immediately.

Tuna Steak

Prep time: 10 minutes | Cook time: 12 minutes | Serves 4

455 g tuna steaks, boneless and cubed
1 tablespoon mustard

1 tablespoon avocado oil
1 tablespoon apple cider vinegar

1. Mix avocado oil with mustard and apple cider vinegar.
2. Then brush tuna steaks with mustard mixture and put in the air fryer basket.
3. Cook the fish at 182ºC for 6 minutes per side.

Cod with Jalapeño

Prep time: 5 minutes | Cook time: 14 minutes | Serves 4

4 cod fillets, boneless
1 jalapeño, minced

1 tablespoon avocado oil
½ teaspoon minced garlic

1. In the shallow bowl, mix minced jalapeño, avocado oil, and minced garlic.
2. Put the cod fillets in the air fryer basket in one layer and top with minced jalapeño mixture.
3. Cook the fish at 185ºC for 7 minutes per side.

Trout Amandine with Lemon Butter Sauce

Prep time: 20 minutes | Cook time:8 minutes | Serves 4

Trout Amandine:
65 g toasted almonds
30 g grated Parmesan cheese
1 teaspoon salt
½ teaspoon freshly ground black pepper
2 tablespoons butter, melted
4 trout fillets, or salmon fillets, 110 g each
Cooking spray

Lemon Butter Sauce:
8 tablespoons butter, melted
2 tablespoons freshly squeezed lemon juice
½ teaspoon Worcestershire sauce
½ teaspoon salt
½ teaspoon freshly ground black pepper
¼ teaspoon hot sauce

1. In a blender or food processor, pulse the almonds for 5 to 10 seconds until finely processed. Transfer to a shallow bowl and whisk in the Parmesan cheese, salt, and pepper. Place the melted butter in another shallow bowl.
2. One at a time, dip the fish in the melted butter, then the almond mixture, coating thoroughly.
3. Preheat the air fryer to 150ºC. Line the air fryer basket with baking paper.
4. Place the coated fish on the baking paper and spritz with oil.
5. Bake for 4 minutes. Flip the fish, spritz it with oil, and bake for 4 minutes more until the fish flakes easily with a fork.
6. In a small bowl, whisk the butter, lemon juice, Worcestershire sauce, salt, pepper, and hot sauce until blended.
7. Serve with the fish.

Black Cod with Grapes and Kale

Prep time: 10 minutes | Cook time: 15 minutes | Serves 2

2 fillets of black cod, 200 g each
Salt and freshly ground black pepper, to taste
Olive oil
150 g grapes, halved
1 small bulb fennel, sliced ¼-inch thick

65 g pecans
200 g shredded kale
2 teaspoons white balsamic vinegar or white wine vinegar
2 tablespoons extra-virgin olive oil

1. Preheat the air fryer to 204ºC.
2. Season the cod fillets with salt and pepper and drizzle, brush or spray a little olive oil on top. Place the fish, presentation side up (skin side down), into the air fryer basket. Air fry for 10 minutes.
3. When the fish has finished cooking, remove the fillets to a side plate and loosely tent with foil to rest.
4. Toss the grapes, fennel and pecans in a bowl with a drizzle of olive oil and season with salt and pepper. Add the grapes, fennel and pecans to the air fryer basket and air fry for 5 minutes, shaking the basket once during the cooking time.
5. Transfer the grapes, fennel and pecans to a bowl with the kale. Dress the kale with the balsamic vinegar and olive oil, season to taste with salt and pepper and serve alongside the cooked fish.

Mediterranean-Style Cod

Prep time: 5 minutes | Cook time: 12 minutes | Serves 4

4 cod fillets, 170 g each
3 tablespoons fresh lemon juice
1 tablespoon olive oil
¼ teaspoon salt

6 cherry tomatoes, halved
45 g pitted and sliced kalamata olives

1. Place cod into an ungreased round nonstick baking dish. Pour lemon juice into dish and drizzle cod with olive oil. Sprinkle with salt. Place tomatoes and olives around baking dish in between fillets.
2. Place dish into air fryer basket. Adjust the temperature to 176ºC and bake for 12 minutes, carefully turning cod halfway through cooking. Fillets will be lightly browned, easily flake, and have an internal temperature of at least 64ºC when done. Serve warm.

Salmon with Cauliflower

Prep time: 10 minutes | Cook time: 25 minutes | Serves 4

455 g salmon fillet, diced
100 g cauliflower, shredded
1 tablespoon dried coriander

1 tablespoon coconut oil, melted
1 teaspoon ground turmeric
60 ml coconut cream

1. Mix salmon with cauliflower, dried cilantro, ground turmeric, coconut cream, and coconut oil.
2. Transfer the salmon mixture into the air fryer and cook the meal at 176°C for 25 minutes. Stir the meal every 5 minutes to avoid the burning.

Calamari with Hot Sauce

Prep time: 10 minutes | Cook time: 6 minutes | Serves 2

280 g calamari, trimmed
2 tablespoons hot sauce

1 tablespoon avocado oil

1. Slice the calamari and sprinkle with avocado oil.
2. Put the calamari in the air fryer and cook at 204°C for 3 minutes per side.
3. Then transfer the calamari in the serving plate and sprinkle with hot sauce.

Tilapia Sandwiches with Tartar Sauce

Prep time: 8 minutes | Cook time: 17 minutes | Serves 4

160 g mayonnaise
2 tablespoons dried minced onion
1 dill pickle spear, finely chopped
2 teaspoons pickle juice
¼ teaspoon salt
⅛ teaspoon freshly ground black pepper

40 g plain flour
1 egg, lightly beaten
200 g panko bread crumbs
2 teaspoons lemon pepper
4 (170 g) tilapia fillets
Olive oil spray
4 soft sub rolls
4 lettuce leaves

1. To make the tartar sauce, in a small bowl, whisk the mayonnaise, dried onion, pickle, pickle juice, salt, and pepper until blended. Refrigerate while you make the fish.
2. Scoop the flour onto a plate; set aside.
3. Put the beaten egg in a medium shallow bowl.
4. On another plate, stir together the panko and lemon pepper.
5. Insert the crisper plate into the basket and the basket into the unit. Preheat the unit to 204°C.
6. Dredge the tilapia fillets in the flour, in the egg, and press into the panko mixture to coat.
7. Once the unit is preheated, spray the crisper plate with olive oil and place a baking paper liner into the basket. Place the prepared fillets on the liner in a single layer. Lightly spray the fillets with olive oil.
8. cook for 8 minutes, remove the basket, carefully flip the fillets, and spray them with more olive oil. Reinsert the basket to resume cooking.
9. When the cooking is complete, the fillets should be golden and crispy and a food thermometer should register 64°C. Place each cooked fillet in a sub roll, top with a little bit of tartar sauce and lettuce, and serve.

Italian Baked Cod

Prep time: 5 minutes | Cook time: 12 minutes | Serves 4

4 cod fillets, 170 g each
2 tablespoons salted butter, melted
1 teaspoon Italian seasoning

¼ teaspoon salt
120 ml tomato-based pasta sauce

1. Place cod into an ungreased round nonstick baking dish. Pour butter over cod and sprinkle with Italian seasoning and salt. Top with pasta sauce.
2. Place dish into air fryer basket. Adjust the temperature to 176°C and bake for 12 minutes. Fillets will be lightly browned, easily flake, and have an internal temperature of at least 64°C when done. Serve warm.

Blackened Fish

Prep time: 15 minutes | Cook time: 8 minutes | Serves 4

1 large egg, beaten
Blackened seasoning, as needed
2 tablespoons light brown sugar

4 tilapia fillets, 110g each
Cooking spray

1. In a shallow bowl, place the beaten egg. In a second shallow bowl, stir together the Blackened seasoning and the brown sugar.
2. One at a time, dip the fish fillets in the egg, then the brown sugar mixture, coating thoroughly.
3. Preheat the air fryer to 150°C. Line the air fryer basket with baking paper.
4. Place the coated fish on the baking paper and spritz with oil.
5. Bake for 4 minutes. Flip the fish, spritz it with oil, and bake for 4 to 6 minutes more until the fish is white inside and flakes easily with a fork.
6. Serve immediately.

Oregano Tilapia Fingers

Prep time: 15 minutes | Cook time: 9 minutes | Serves 4

455 g tilapia fillet
60 g coconut flour
2 eggs, beaten

½ teaspoon ground paprika
1 teaspoon dried oregano
1 teaspoon avocado oil

1. Cut the tilapia fillets into fingers and sprinkle with ground paprika and dried oregano.
2. Then dip the tilapia fingers in eggs and coat in the coconut flour.
3. Sprinkle fish fingers with avocado oil and cook in the air fryer at 188ºC for 9 minutes.

chilli Prawns

Prep time: 10 minutes | Cook time: 8 minutes | Serves 2

8 prawns, peeled and deveined
Salt and black pepper, to taste
½ teaspoon ground cayenne pepper

½ teaspoon garlic powder
½ teaspoon ground cumin
½ teaspoon red chilli flakes
Cooking spray

1. Preheat the air fryer to 172ºC. Spritz the air fryer basket with cooking spray.
2. Toss the remaining ingredients in a large bowl until the prawns are well coated.
3. Spread the coated prawns evenly in the basket and spray them with cooking spray.
4. Air fry for 8 minutes, flipping the prawns halfway through, or until the prawns are pink.
5. Remove the prawns from the basket to a plate.

Swordfish Skewers with Caponata

Prep time: 15 minutes | Cook time: 20 minutes | Serves 2

280 g small Italian aubergine, cut into 1-inch pieces
170 g cherry tomatoes
3 spring onions, cut into 2 inches long
2 tablespoons extra-virgin olive oil, divided
Salt and pepper, to taste
340 g skinless swordfish steaks, 1¼ inches thick, cut into 1-inch pieces

2 teaspoons honey, divided
2 teaspoons ground coriander, divided
1 teaspoon grated lemon zest, divided
1 teaspoon juice
4 (6-inch) wooden skewers
1 garlic clove, minced
½ teaspoon ground cumin
1 tablespoon chopped fresh basil

1. Preheat the air fryer to 204ºC.
2. Toss aubergine, tomatoes, and spring onions with 1 tablespoon oil, ¼ teaspoon salt, and ⅛ teaspoon pepper in bowl; transfer to air fryer basket. Air fry until aubergine is softened and browned and tomatoes have begun to burst, about 14 minutes, tossing halfway through cooking. Transfer vegetables to cutting board and set aside to cool slightly.
3. Pat swordfish dry with paper towels. Combine 1 teaspoon oil, 1 teaspoon honey, 1 teaspoon coriander, ½ teaspoon lemon zest, ⅛ teaspoon salt, and pinch pepper in a clean bowl. Add swordfish and toss to coat. Thread swordfish onto skewers, leaving about ¼ inch between each piece (3 or 4 pieces per skewer).
4. Arrange skewers in air fryer basket, spaced evenly apart. (Skewers may overlap slightly.) Return basket to air fryer and air fry until swordfish is browned and registers 140ºF (60ºC), 6 to 8 minutes, flipping and rotating skewers halfway through cooking.
5. Meanwhile, combine remaining 2 teaspoons oil, remaining 1 teaspoon honey, remaining 1 teaspoon coriander, remaining ½ teaspoon lemon zest, lemon juice, garlic, cumin, ¼ teaspoon salt, and ⅛ teaspoon pepper in large bowl. Microwave, stirring once, until fragrant, about 30 seconds. Coarsely chop the cooked vegetables, transfer to bowl with dressing, along with any accumulated juices, and gently toss to combine. Stir in basil and season with salt and pepper to taste. Serve skewers with caponata.

Classic Prawns Empanadas

Prep time: 10 minutes | Cook time: 8 minutes | Serves 5

230 g raw prawns, peeled, deveined and chopped
1 small chopped red onion
1 spring onion, chopped
2 garlic cloves, minced
2 tablespoons minced red bell pepper
2 tablespoons chopped fresh coriander

½ tablespoon fresh lime juice
¼ teaspoon sweet paprika
⅛ teaspoon kosher salt
⅛ teaspoon crushed red pepper flakes (optional)
1 large egg, beaten
10 frozen Goya Empanada Discos, thawed
Cooking spray

1. In a medium bowl, combine the prawns, red onion, spring onion, garlic, bell pepper, coriander, lime juice, paprika, salt, and pepper flakes (if using).
2. In a small bowl, beat the egg with 1 teaspoon water until smooth.
3. Place an empanada disc on a work surface and put 2 tablespoons of the prawn mixture in the center. Brush the outer edges of the disc with the egg wash. Fold the disc over and gently press the edges to seal. Use a fork and press around the edges to crimp and seal completely. Brush the tops of the empanadas with the egg wash.
4. Preheat the air fryer to 192ºC.
5. Spray the bottom of the air fryer basket with cooking spray to prevent sticking. Working in batches, arrange a single layer of the empanadas in the air fryer basket and air fry for about 8 minutes, flipping halfway, until golden brown and crispy.
6. Serve hot.

Golden Beer-Battered Cod

Prep time: 5 minutes | Cook time: 15 minutes | Serves 4

2 eggs

240 ml malty beer

120 g plain flour

60 g cornflour

1 teaspoon garlic powder

Salt and pepper, to taste

4 cod fillets, 110 g each

Cooking spray

1. Preheat the air fryer to 204°C.
2. In a shallow bowl, beat together the eggs with the beer. In another shallow bowl, thoroughly combine the flour and cornflour. Sprinkle with the garlic powder, salt, and pepper.
3. Dredge each cod fillet in the flour mixture, then in the egg mixture. Dip each piece of fish in the flour mixture a second time.
4. Spritz the air fryer basket with cooking spray. Arrange the cod fillets in the basket in a single layer.
5. Air fry in batches for 15 minutes until the cod reaches an internal temperature of 64°C on a meat thermometer and the outside is crispy. Flip the fillets halfway through the cooking time.
6. Let the fish cool for 5 minutes and serve.

Cajun Salmon

Prep time: 5 minutes | Cook time: 7 minutes | Serves 2

2 salmon fillets, skin removed, 100 g each

2 tablespoons unsalted butter, melted

⅛ teaspoon ground cayenne pepper

½ teaspoon garlic powder

1 teaspoon paprika

¼ teaspoon ground black pepper

1. Brush each fillet with butter.
2. Combine remaining ingredients in a small bowl and then rub onto fish. Place fillets into the air fryer basket.
3. Adjust the temperature to 200°C and air fry for 7 minutes.
4. When fully cooked, internal temperature will be 64°C. Serve immediately.

Bacon-Wrapped Scallops

Prep time: 5 minutes | Cook time: 10 minutes | Serves 4

8 sea scallops, 30 g each, cleaned and patted dry

8 slices bacon

¼ teaspoon salt

¼ teaspoon ground black pepper

1. Wrap each scallop in 1 slice bacon and secure with a toothpick. Sprinkle with salt and pepper.
2. Place scallops into ungreased air fryer basket. Adjust the temperature to 182°C and air fry for 10 minutes. Scallops will be opaque and firm, and have an internal temperature of 56°C when done. Serve warm.

Chapter 6 Vegetables and Sides

Chapter 6 Vegetables and Sides

Sweet-and-Sour Brussels Sprouts

Prep time: 10 minutes | Cook time: 20 minutes | Serves 2

70 g Thai sweet chili sauce
2 tablespoons black vinegar or balsamic vinegar
½ teaspoon hot sauce, such as Tabasco
230 g Brussels sprouts, trimmed (large sprouts halved)

2 small shallots, cut into ¼-inch-thick slices
coarse sea salt and freshly ground black pepper, to taste
2 teaspoons lightly packed fresh coriander leaves

1. In a large bowl, whisk together the chili sauce, vinegar, and hot sauce. Add the Brussels sprouts and shallots, season with salt and pepper, and toss to combine. Scrape the Brussels sprouts and sauce into a cake pan.
2. Place the pan in the air fryer and roast at 192ºC, stirring every 5 minutes, until the Brussels sprouts are tender and the sauce is reduced to a sticky glaze, about 20 minutes.
3. Remove the pan from the air fryer and transfer the Brussels sprouts to plates. Sprinkle with the coriander and serve warm.

Breaded Green Tomatoes

Prep time: 15 minutes | Cook time: 30 minutes | Serves 4

60 g plain flour
2 eggs
60 g semolina
60 g panko bread crumbs
1 teaspoon garlic powder

Salt and freshly ground black pepper, to taste
2 green tomatoes, cut into ½-inch-thick rounds
Cooking oil spray

1. Place the flour in a small bowl.
2. In another small bowl, beat the eggs.
3. In a third small bowl, stir together the semolina, panko, and garlic powder. Season with salt and pepper.
4. Dip each tomato slice into the flour, the egg, and finally the semolina mixture to coat.
5. Insert the crisper plate into the basket and the basket into the unit. Preheat the unit by selecting AIR FRY, setting the temperature to 200ºC, and setting the time to 3 minutes. Select START/STOP to begin.
6. Once the unit is preheated, spray the crisper plate and the basket with cooking oil. Working in batches, place the tomato slices in the air fryer in a single layer. Do not stack them. Spray the tomato slices with the cooking oil.

7. Select AIR FRY, set the temperature to 200ºC, and set the time to 10 minutes. Select START/STOP to begin.
8. After 5 minutes, use tongs to flip the tomatoes. Resume cooking for 4 to 5 minutes, or until crisp.
9. When the cooking is complete, transfer the fried green tomatoes to a plate. Repeat steps 6, 7, and 8 for the remaining tomatoes.

Butter and Garlic Fried Cabbage

Prep time: 5 minutes | Cook time: 9 minutes | Serves 2

Oil, for spraying
½ head cabbage, cut into bite-size pieces
2 tablespoons unsalted butter, melted

1 teaspoon granulated garlic
½ teaspoon coarse sea salt
¼ teaspoon freshly ground black pepper

1. Line the air fryer basket with parchment and spray lightly with oil.
2. In a large bowl, mix together the cabbage, butter, garlic, salt, and black pepper until evenly coated.
3. Transfer the cabbage to the prepared basket and spray lightly with oil.
4. Air fry at 192ºC for 5 minutes, toss, and cook for another 3 to 4 minutes, or until lightly crispy.

Dinner Rolls

Prep time: 10 minutes | Cook time: 12 minutes | Serves 6

225 g shredded Mozzarella cheese
30 g full-fat cream cheese
95 g blanched finely ground

almond flour
40 g ground flaxseed
½ teaspoon baking powder
1 large egg

1. Place Mozzarella, cream cheese, and almond flour in a large microwave-safe bowl. Microwave for 1 minute. Mix until smooth.
2. Add flaxseed, baking powder, and egg until fully combined and smooth. Microwave an additional 15 seconds if it becomes too firm.
3. Separate the dough into six pieces and roll into balls. Place the balls into the air fryer basket.
4. Adjust the temperature to 160ºC and air fry for 12 minutes.
5. Allow rolls to cool completely before serving.

Curried Fruit

Prep time: 10 minutes | Cook time: 20 minutes | Serves 6 to 8

210 g cubed fresh pineapple
200 g cubed fresh pear (firm, not overly ripe)
230 g frozen peaches, thawed

425 g can dark, sweet, pitted cherries with juice
2 tablespoons brown sugar
1 teaspoon curry powder

1. Combine all ingredients in large bowl. Stir gently to mix in the sugar and curry.
2. Pour into a baking pan and bake at 180ºC for 10 minutes.
3. Stir fruit and cook 10 more minutes.
4. Serve hot.

Crispy Garlic Sliced Aubergine

Prep time: 5 minutes | Cook time: 25 minutes | Serves 4

1 egg
1 tablespoon water
60 g whole wheat bread crumbs
1 teaspoon garlic powder
½ teaspoon dried oregano

½ teaspoon salt
½ teaspoon paprika
1 medium aubergine, sliced into ¼-inch-thick rounds
1 tablespoon olive oil

1. Preheat the air fryer to 180ºC.
2. In a medium shallow bowl, beat together the egg and water until frothy.
3. In a separate medium shallow bowl, mix together bread crumbs, garlic powder, oregano, salt, and paprika.
4. Dip each aubergine slice into the egg mixture, then into the bread crumb mixture, coating the outside with crumbs. Place the slices in a single layer in the bottom of the air fryer basket.
5. Drizzle the tops of the aubergine slices with the olive oil, then fry for 15 minutes. Turn each slice and cook for an additional 10 minutes.

Courgette Fritters

Prep time: 10 minutes | Cook time: 10 minutes | Serves 4

2 courgette, grated (about 450 g)
1 teaspoon salt
25 g almond flour
20 g grated Parmesan cheese
1 large egg
¼ teaspoon dried thyme

¼ teaspoon ground turmeric
¼ teaspoon freshly ground black pepper
1 tablespoon olive oil
½ lemon, sliced into wedges

1. Preheat the air fryer to 200ºC. Cut a piece of parchment paper to fit slightly smaller than the bottom of the air fryer.
2. Place the courgette in a large colander and sprinkle with the salt.

Let sit for 5 to 10 minutes. Squeeze as much liquid as you can from the courgette and place in a large mixing bowl. Add the almond flour, Parmesan, egg, thyme, turmeric, and black pepper. Stir gently until thoroughly combined.
3. Shape the mixture into 8 patties and arrange on the parchment paper. Brush lightly with the olive oil. Pausing halfway through the cooking time to turn the patties, air fry for 10 minutes until golden brown. Serve warm with the lemon wedges.

Rosemary New Potatoes

Prep time: 10 minutes | Cook time: 5 to 6 minutes | Serves 4

3 large red potatoes
¼ teaspoon ground rosemary
¼ teaspoon ground thyme

⅛ teaspoon salt
⅛ teaspoon ground black pepper
2 teaspoons extra-light olive oil

1. Preheat the air fryer to 170ºC. 2. Place potatoes in large bowl and sprinkle with rosemary, thyme, salt, and pepper.
3. Stir with a spoon to distribute seasonings evenly.
4. Add oil to potatoes and stir again to coat well.
5. Air fry at 170ºC for 4 minutes. Stir and break apart any that have stuck together.
6. Cook an additional 1 to 2 minutes or until fork-tender.

Garlic-Parmesan Crispy Baby Potatoes

Prep time: 10 minutes | Cook time: 15 minutes | Serves 4

Oil, for spraying
450 g baby potatoes
45 g grated Parmesan cheese, divided
3 tablespoons olive oil
2 teaspoons garlic powder
½ teaspoon onion powder

½ teaspoon salt
¼ teaspoon freshly ground black pepper
¼ teaspoon paprika
2 tablespoons chopped fresh parsley, for garnish

1. Line the air fryer basket with parchment and spray lightly with oil.
2. Rinse the potatoes, pat dry with paper towels, and place in a large bowl.
3. In a small bowl, mix together 45 g of Parmesan cheese, the olive oil, garlic, onion powder, salt, black pepper, and paprika. Pour the mixture over the potatoes and toss to coat.
4. Transfer the potatoes to the prepared basket and spread them out in an even layer, taking care to keep them from touching. You may need to work in batches, depending on the size of your air fryer.
5. Air fry at 200ºC for 15 minutes, stirring after 7 to 8 minutes, or until easily pierced with a fork. Continue to cook for another 1 to 2 minutes, if needed.
6. Sprinkle with the parsley and the remaining Parmesan cheese and serve.

Roasted Grape Tomatoes and Asparagus

Prep time: 5 minutes | Cook time: 12 minutes | Serves 6

400 g grape tomatoes

1 bunch asparagus, trimmed

2 tablespoons olive oil

3 garlic cloves, minced

½ teaspoon coarse sea salt

1. Preheat the air fryer to 192°C.
2. In a large bowl, combine all of the ingredients, tossing until the vegetables are well coated with oil.
3. Pour the vegetable mixture into the air fryer basket and spread into a single layer, then roast for 12 minutes.

Scalloped Potatoes

Prep time: 5 minutes | Cook time: 20 minutes | Serves 4

440 g sliced frozen potatoes, thawed

3 cloves garlic, minced

Pinch salt

Freshly ground black pepper, to taste

180 g double cream

1. Preheat the air fryer to 192°C.
2. Toss the potatoes with the garlic, salt, and black pepper in a baking pan until evenly coated. Pour the double cream over the top.
3. Place the baking pan in the air fryer basket and bake for 15 minutes, or until the potatoes are tender and top is golden brown. Check for doneness and bake for another 5 minutes as needed.
4. Serve hot.

Fried Brussels Sprouts

Prep time: 10 minutes | Cook time: 18 minutes | Serves 4

1 teaspoon plus 1 tablespoon extra-virgin olive oil, divided

2 teaspoons minced garlic

2 tablespoons honey

1 tablespoon sugar

2 tablespoons freshly squeezed lemon juice

2 tablespoons rice vinegar

2 tablespoons sriracha

450 g Brussels sprouts, stems trimmed and any tough leaves removed, rinsed, halved lengthwise, and dried

½ teaspoon salt

Cooking oil spray

1. In a small saucepan over low heat, combine 1 teaspoon of olive oil, the garlic, honey, sugar, lemon juice, vinegar, and sriracha. Cook for 2 to 3 minutes, or until slightly thickened. Remove the pan from the heat, cover, and set aside.
2. Place the Brussels sprouts in a resealable bag or small bowl. Add the remaining olive oil and the salt, and toss to coat.

3. Insert the crisper plate into the basket and the basket into the unit. Preheat the unit by selecting AIR FRY, setting the temperature to 200°C, and setting the time to 3 minutes. Select START/STOP to begin.
4. Once the unit is preheated, spray the crisper plate with cooking oil. Add the Brussels sprouts to the basket.
5. Select AIR FRY, set the temperature to 200°C, and set the time to 15 minutes. Select START/STOP to begin.
6. After 7 or 8 minutes, remove the basket and shake it to toss the sprouts. Reinsert the basket to resume cooking.
7. When the cooking is complete, the leaves should be crispy and light brown and the sprout centres tender.
8. Place the sprouts in a medium serving bowl and drizzle the sauce over the top. Toss to coat, and serve immediately.

Crispy Lemon Artichoke Hearts

Prep time: 10 minutes | Cook time: 15 minutes | Serves 2

1 (425 g) can artichoke hearts in water, drained

1 egg

1 tablespoon water

30 g whole wheat bread crumbs

¼ teaspoon salt

¼ teaspoon paprika

½ lemon

1. Preheat the air fryer to 192°C.
2. In a medium shallow bowl, beat together the egg and water until frothy.
3. In a separate medium shallow bowl, mix together the bread crumbs, salt, and paprika.
4. Dip each artichoke heart into the egg mixture, then into the bread crumb mixture, coating the outside with the crumbs. Place the artichokes hearts in a single layer of the air fryer basket.
5. Fry the artichoke hearts for 15 minutes.
6. Remove the artichokes from the air fryer, and squeeze fresh lemon juice over the top before serving.

Garlic Courgette and Red Peppers

Prep time: 5 minutes | Cook time: 15 minutes | Serves 6

2 medium courgette, cubed

1 red pepper, diced

2 garlic cloves, sliced

2 tablespoons olive oil

½ teaspoon salt

1. Preheat the air fryer to 193°C.
2. In a large bowl, mix together the courgette, bell pepper, and garlic with the olive oil and salt.
3. Pour the mixture into the air fryer basket, and roast for 7 minutes. Shake or stir, then roast for 7 to 8 minutes more.

Balsamic Brussels Sprouts

Prep time: 5 minutes | Cook time: 12 minutes | Serves 4

180 g trimmed and halved fresh Brussels sprouts
2 tablespoons olive oil
¼ teaspoon salt

¼ teaspoon ground black pepper
2 tablespoons balsamic vinegar
2 slices cooked sugar-free bacon, crumbled

1. In a large bowl, toss Brussels sprouts in olive oil, then sprinkle with salt and pepper. Place into ungreased air fryer basket. Adjust the temperature to 192ºC and set the timer for 12 minutes, shaking the basket halfway through cooking. Brussels sprouts will be tender and browned when done.
2. Place sprouts in a large serving dish and drizzle with balsamic vinegar. Sprinkle bacon over top. Serve warm.

Five-Spice Roasted Sweet Potatoes

Prep time: 10 minutes | Cook time: 12 minutes | Serves 4

½ teaspoon ground cinnamon
¼ teaspoon ground cumin
¼ teaspoon paprika
1 teaspoon chili powder
⅛ teaspoon turmeric
½ teaspoon salt (optional)

Freshly ground black pepper, to taste
2 large sweet potatoes, peeled and cut into ¾-inch cubes
1 tablespoon olive oil

1. In a large bowl, mix together cinnamon, cumin, paprika, chili powder, turmeric, salt, and pepper to taste.
2. Add potatoes and stir well.
3. Drizzle the seasoned potatoes with the olive oil and stir until evenly coated.
4. Place seasoned potatoes in a baking pan or an ovenproof dish that fits inside your air fryer basket.
5. Cook for 6 minutes at 200ºC, stop, and stir well.
6. Cook for an additional 6 minutes.

Easy Potato Croquettes

Prep time: 15 minutes | Cook time: 15 minutes | Serves 10

55 g nutritional yeast
300 g boiled potatoes, mashed
1 flax egg
1 tablespoon flour
2 tablespoons chopped chives

Salt and ground black pepper, to taste
2 tablespoons vegetable oil
30 g bread crumbs

1. Preheat the air fryer to 200ºC.

2. In a bowl, combine the nutritional yeast, potatoes, flax egg, flour, and chives. Sprinkle with salt and pepper as desired.
3. In a separate bowl, mix the vegetable oil and bread crumbs to achieve a crumbly consistency.
4. Shape the potato mixture into small balls and dip each one into the bread crumb mixture.
5. Put the croquettes inside the air fryer and air fry for 15 minutes, ensuring the croquettes turn golden brown.
6. Serve immediately.

Cheesy Loaded Broccoli

Prep time: 10 minutes | Cook time: 10 minutes | Serves 2

215 g fresh broccoli florets
1 tablespoon coconut oil
¼ teaspoon salt
120 g shredded sharp Cheddar cheese

60 g sour cream
4 slices cooked sugar-free bacon, crumbled
1 medium spring onion, trimmed and sliced on the bias

1. Place broccoli into ungreased air fryer basket, drizzle with coconut oil, and sprinkle with salt. Adjust the temperature to 180ºC and roast for 8 minutes. Shake basket three times during cooking to avoid burned spots.
2. Sprinkle broccoli with Cheddar and cook for 2 additional minutes. When done, cheese will be melted and broccoli will be tender.
3. Serve warm in a large serving dish, topped with sour cream, crumbled bacon, and spring onion slices.

Lemon-Thyme Asparagus

Prep time: 5 minutes | Cook time: 4 to 8 minutes | Serves 4

450 g asparagus, woody ends trimmed off
1 tablespoon avocado oil
½ teaspoon dried thyme or ½ tablespoon chopped fresh thyme
Sea salt and freshly ground

black pepper, to taste
60 g goat cheese, crumbled
Zest and juice of 1 lemon
Flaky sea salt, for serving (optional)

1. In a medium bowl, toss together the asparagus, avocado oil, and thyme, and season with sea salt and pepper.
2. Place the asparagus in the air fryer basket in a single layer. Set the air fryer to 200ºC and air fry for 4 to 8 minutes, to your desired doneness.
3. Transfer to a serving platter. Top with the goat cheese, lemon zest, and lemon juice. If desired, season with a pinch of flaky salt.

Garlic Parmesan-Roasted Cauliflower

Prep time: 5 minutes | Cook time: 15 minutes | Serves 6

1 medium head cauliflower, leaves and core removed, cut into florets

2 tablespoons salted butter, melted

½ tablespoon salt

2 cloves garlic, peeled and finely minced

45 g grated Parmesan cheese, divided

1. Toss cauliflower in a large bowl with butter. Sprinkle with salt, garlic, and ½ of the Parmesan.
2. Place florets into ungreased air fryer basket. Adjust the temperature to 180°C and roast for 15 minutes, shaking basket halfway through cooking. Cauliflower will be browned at the edges and tender when done.
3. Transfer florets to a large serving dish and sprinkle with remaining Parmesan. Serve warm.

Chapter 7 Beef, Pork, and Lamb

Chapter 7 Beef, Pork, and Lamb

Garlic-Marinated Bavette Steak

Prep time: 30 minutes | Cook time: 8 to 10 minutes | Serves 6

120 ml avocado oil
60 ml soy sauce or tamari
1 shallot, minced
1 tablespoon minced garlic
2 tablespoons chopped fresh oregano, or 2 teaspoons dried

1½ teaspoons sea salt
1 teaspoon freshly ground black pepper
¼ teaspoon red pepper flakes
900 g bavette or skirt steak

1. In a blender, combine the avocado oil, soy sauce, shallot, garlic, oregano, salt, black pepper, and red pepper flakes. Process until smooth.
2. Place the steak in a zip-top plastic bag or shallow dish with the marinade. Seal the bag or cover the dish and marinate in the refrigerator for at least 2 hours or overnight.
3. Remove the steak from the bag and discard the marinade.
4. Set the air fryer to 204°C. Place the steak in the air fryer basket (if needed, cut into sections and work in batches). Air fry for 4 to 6 minutes, flip the steak, and cook for another 4 minutes or until the internal temperature reaches 49°C in the thickest part for medium-rare (or as desired).

Greek Lamb Pitta Pockets

Prep time: 15 minutes | Cook time: 6 minutes | Serves 4

Dressing:
235 ml plain yogurt
1 tablespoon lemon juice
1 teaspoon dried dill, crushed
1 teaspoon ground oregano
½ teaspoon salt
Meatballs:
230 g lamb mince
1 tablespoon diced onion
1 teaspoon dried parsley
1 teaspoon dried dill, crushed
¼ teaspoon oregano

¼ teaspoon coriander
¼ teaspoon ground cumin
¼ teaspoon salt
4 pitta halves
Suggested Toppings:
1 red onion, slivered
1 medium cucumber, deseeded, thinly sliced
Crumbled feta cheese
Sliced black olives
Chopped fresh peppers

1. Preheat the air fryer to 200°C.
2. Stir the dressing ingredients together in a small bowl and refrigerate while preparing lamb.
3. Combine all meatball ingredients in a large bowl and stir to distribute seasonings.

4. Shape meat mixture into 12 small meatballs, rounded or slightly flattened if you prefer.
5. Transfer the meatballs in the preheated air fryer and air fry for 6 minutes, until well done. Remove and drain on paper towels.
6. To serve, pile meatballs and the choice of toppings in pitta pockets and drizzle with dressing.

Greek Lamb Rack

Prep time: 5 minutes | Cook time: 10 minutes | Serves 4

60 ml freshly squeezed lemon juice
1 teaspoon oregano
2 teaspoons minced fresh rosemary
1 teaspoon minced fresh thyme

2 tablespoons minced garlic
Salt and freshly ground black pepper, to taste
2 to 4 tablespoons olive oil
1 lamb rib rack (7 to 8 ribs)

1. Preheat the air fryer to 182°C.
2. In a small mixing bowl, combine the lemon juice, oregano, rosemary, thyme, garlic, salt, pepper, and olive oil and mix well.
3. Rub the mixture over the lamb, covering all the meat. Put the rack of lamb in the air fryer. Roast for 10 minutes. Flip the rack halfway through.
4. After 10 minutes, measure the internal temperature of the rack of lamb reaches at least 64°C.
5. Serve immediately.

Italian Sausage Links

Prep time: 10 minutes | Cook time: 24 minutes | Serves 4

1 pepper (any color), sliced
1 medium onion, sliced
1 tablespoon avocado oil
1 teaspoon Italian seasoning

Sea salt and freshly ground black pepper, to taste
450 g Italian-seasoned sausage links

1. Place the pepper and onion in a medium bowl, and toss with the avocado oil, Italian seasoning, and salt and pepper to taste.
2. Set the air fryer to 204°C. Put the vegetables in the air fryer basket and cook for 12 minutes.
3. Push the vegetables to the side of the basket and arrange the sausage links in the bottom of the basket in a single layer. Spoon the vegetables over the sausages. Cook for 12 minutes, tossing halfway through, until an instant-read thermometer inserted into the sausage reads 72°C.

Beef Mince Taco Rolls

Prep time: 20 minutes | Cook time: 10 minutes | Serves 4

230 g 80/20 beef mince	2 tablespoons chopped coriander
80 ml water	355 ml shredded Mozzarella
1 tablespoon chili powder	cheese
2 teaspoons cumin	120 ml blanched finely ground
½ teaspoon garlic powder	almond flour
¼ teaspoon dried oregano	60 g full-fat cream cheese
60 ml tinned diced tomatoes	1 large egg

1. In a medium skillet over medium heat, brown the beef mince about 7 to 10 minutes. When meat is fully cooked, drain.
2. Add water to skillet and stir in chili powder, cumin, garlic powder, oregano, and tomatoes. Add coriander. Bring to a boil, then reduce heat to simmer for 3 minutes.
3. In a large microwave-safe bowl, place Mozzarella, almond flour, cream cheese, and egg. Microwave for 1 minute. Stir the mixture quickly until smooth ball of dough forms.
4. Cut a piece of parchment for your work surface. Press the dough into a large rectangle on the parchment, wetting your hands to prevent the dough from sticking as necessary. Cut the dough into eight rectangles.
5. On each rectangle place a few spoons of the meat mixture. Fold the short ends of each roll toward the center and roll the length as you would a burrito.
6. Cut a piece of parchment to fit your air fryer basket. Place taco rolls onto the parchment and place into the air fryer basket.
7. Adjust the temperature to 182°C and air fry for 10 minutes.
8. Flip halfway through the cooking time.
9. Allow to cool 10 minutes before serving.

Spicy Lamb Sirloin Chops

Prep time: 30 minutes | Cook time: 15 minutes | Serves 4

½ brown onion, coarsely chopped	1 teaspoon ground cinnamon
4 coin-size slices peeled fresh ginger	1 teaspoon ground turmeric
	½ to 1 teaspoon cayenne pepper
5 garlic cloves	½ teaspoon ground cardamom
1 teaspoon garam masala	1 teaspoon coarse or flaky salt
1 teaspoon ground fennel	450 g lamb sirloin chops

1. In a blender, combine the onion, ginger, garlic, garam masala, fennel, cinnamon, turmeric, cayenne, cardamom, and salt. Pulse until the onion is finely minced and the mixture forms a thick paste, 3 to 4 minutes.
2. Place the lamb chops in a large bowl. Slash the meat and fat with a sharp knife several times to allow the marinade to penetrate better. Add the spice paste to the bowl and toss the lamb to coat. Marinate

at room temperature for 30 minutes or cover and refrigerate for up to 24 hours.
3. Place the lamb chops in a single layer in the air fryer basket. Set the air fryer to 164°C for 15 minutes, turning the chops halfway through the cooking time. Use a meat thermometer to ensure the lamb has reached an internal temperature of 64°C (medium-rare).

Easy Beef Satay

Prep time: 30 minutes | Cook time: 8 minutes | Serves 4

450 g beef bavette or skirt steak, thinly sliced into long strips	1 tablespoon minced garlic
	1 tablespoon sugar
2 tablespoons vegetable oil	1 teaspoon Sriracha or other hot
1 tablespoon fish sauce	sauce
1 tablespoon soy sauce	1 teaspoon ground coriander
1 tablespoon minced fresh ginger	120 ml chopped fresh coriander
	60 ml chopped roasted peanuts

1. Place the beef strips in a large bowl or resealable plastic bag. Add the vegetable oil, fish sauce, soy sauce, ginger, garlic, sugar, Sriracha, coriander, and 60 ml of the fresh coriander to the bag. Seal and massage the bag to thoroughly coat and combine. Marinate at room temperature for 30 minutes, or cover and refrigerate for up to 24 hours.
2. Using tongs, remove the beef strips from the bag and lay them flat in the air fryer basket, minimizing overlap as much as possible; discard the marinade. Set the air fryer to 204°C for 8 minutes, turning the beef strips halfway through the cooking time.
3. Transfer the meat to a serving platter. Sprinkle with the remaining 60 ml coriander and the peanuts. Serve.

Southern Chili

Prep time: 20 minutes | Cook time: 25 minutes | Serves 4

450 g beef mince (85% lean)	1 (425 g) can red kidney beans,
235 ml minced onion	rinsed and drained
1 (794 g) can tomato purée	60 ml Chili seasoning
1 (425 g) can diced tomatoes	

1. Preheat the air fryer to 204°C.
2. In a baking pan, mix the mince and onion. Place the pan in the air fryer.
3. Cook for 4 minutes. Stir and cook for 4 minutes more until browned. Remove the pan from the fryer. Drain the meat and transfer to a large bowl.
4. Reduce the air fryer temperature to 176°C.
5. To the bowl with the meat, add in the tomato purée, diced tomatoes, kidney beans, and Chili seasoning. Mix well. Pour the mixture into the baking pan.
6. Cook for 25 minutes, stirring every 10 minutes, until thickened.

Chorizo and Beef Burger

340 g 80/20 beef mince
110 g Mexican-style chorizo crumb
60 ml chopped onion
5 slices pickled jalapeños,

chopped
2 teaspoons chili powder
1 teaspoon minced garlic
¼ teaspoon cumin

1. In a large bowl, mix all ingredients. Divide the mixture into four sections and form them into burger patties.
2. Place burger patties into the air fryer basket, working in batches if necessary.
3. Adjust the temperature to 192°C and air fry for 15 minutes.
4. Flip the patties halfway through the cooking time. Serve warm.

Blue Cheese Steak Salad

2 tablespoons balsamic vinegar
2 tablespoons red wine vinegar
1 tablespoon Dijon mustard
1 tablespoon granulated sweetener
1 teaspoon minced garlic
Sea salt and freshly ground black pepper, to taste

180 ml extra-virgin olive oil
450 g boneless rump steak
Avocado oil spray
1 small red onion, cut into ¼-inch-thick rounds
170 g baby spinach
120 ml cherry tomatoes, halved
85 g blue cheese, crumbled

1. In a blender, combine the balsamic vinegar, red wine vinegar, Dijon mustard, sweetener, and garlic. Season with salt and pepper and process until smooth. With the blender running, drizzle in the olive oil. Process until well combined. Transfer to a jar with a tight-fitting lid, and refrigerate until ready to serve (it will keep for up to 2 weeks).
2. Season the steak with salt and pepper and let sit at room temperature for at least 45 minutes, time permitting.
3. Set the air fryer to 204°C. Spray the steak with oil and place it in the air fryer basket. Air fry for 6 minutes. Flip the steak and spray it with more oil. Air fry for 6 minutes more for medium-rare or until the steak is done to your liking.
4. Transfer the steak to a plate, tent with a piece of aluminum foil, and allow it to rest.
5. Spray the onion slices with oil and place them in the air fryer basket. Cook at 204°C for 5 minutes. Flip the onion slices and spray them with more oil. Air fry for 5 minutes more.
6. Slice the steak diagonally into thin strips. Place the spinach, cherry tomatoes, onion slices, and steak in a large bowl. Toss with the desired amount of dressing. Sprinkle with crumbled blue cheese and serve.

Mongolian Style Beef

Oil, for spraying
60 ml cornflour
450 g bavette or skirt steak, thinly sliced
180 ml packed light brown sugar
120 ml soy sauce

2 teaspoons toasted sesame oil
1 tablespoon minced garlic
½ teaspoon ground ginger
120 ml water
Cooked white rice or ramen noodles, for serving

1. Line the air fryer basket with parchment and spray lightly with oil.
2. Place the cornflour in a bowl and dredge the steak until evenly coated. Shake off any excess cornflour.
3. Place the steak in the prepared basket and spray lightly with oil.
4. Roast at 200°C for 5 minutes, flip, and cook for another 5 minutes.
5. In a small saucepan, combine the brown sugar, soy sauce, sesame oil, garlic, ginger, and water and bring to a boil over medium-high heat, stirring frequently. Remove from the heat.
6. Transfer the meat to the sauce and toss until evenly coated. Let sit for about 5 minutes so the steak absorbs the flavors. Serve with white rice or ramen noodles.

Steak Gyro Platter

450 g bavette or skirt steak
1 teaspoon garlic powder
1 teaspoon ground cumin
½ teaspoon sea salt
½ teaspoon freshly ground black pepper
140 g shredded romaine lettuce
120 ml crumbled feta cheese

120 ml peeled and diced cucumber
80 ml sliced red onion
60 ml seeded and diced tomato
2 tablespoons pitted and sliced black olives
Tzatziki sauce, for serving

1. Pat the steak dry with paper towels. In a small bowl, combine the garlic powder, cumin, salt, and pepper. Sprinkle this mixture all over the steak, and allow the steak to rest at room temperature for 45 minutes.
2. Preheat the air fryer to 204°C. Place the steak in the air fryer basket and air fry for 4 minutes. Flip the steak and cook 4 to 6 minutes more, until an instant-read thermometer reads 49°C at the thickest point for medium-rare (or as desired). Remove the steak from the air fryer and let it rest for 5 minutes.
3. Divide the romaine among plates. Top with the feta, cucumber, red onion, tomato, and olives.

London Broil with Herb Butter

Prep time: 30 minutes | Cook time: 20 to 25 minutes | Serves 4

680 g bavette or skirt steak
60 ml olive oil
2 tablespoons balsamic vinegar
1 tablespoon Worcestershire sauce
4 cloves garlic, minced
Herb Butter:
6 tablespoons unsalted butter,
softened
1 tablespoon chopped fresh parsley
¼ teaspoon salt
¼ teaspoon dried ground rosemary or thyme
¼ teaspoon garlic powder
Pinch of red pepper flakes

1. Place the beef in a gallon-size resealable bag. In a small bowl, whisk together the olive oil, balsamic vinegar, Worcestershire sauce, and garlic. Pour the marinade over the beef, massaging gently to coat, and seal the bag. Let sit at room temperature for an hour or refrigerate overnight.
2. To make the herb butter: In a small bowl, mix the butter with the parsley, salt, rosemary, garlic powder, and red pepper flakes until smooth. Cover and refrigerate until ready to use.
3. Preheat the air fryer to 204°C.
4. Remove the beef from the marinade (discard the marinade) and place the beef in the air fryer basket. Pausing halfway through the cooking time to turn the meat, air fry for 20 to 25 minutes, until a thermometer inserted into the thickest part indicates the desired doneness, 52°C (rare) to 64°C (medium). Let the beef rest for 10 minutes before slicing. Serve topped with the herb butter.

Air Fried Beef Satay with Peanut Dipping Sauce

Prep time: 30 minutes | Cook time: 5 to 7 minutes | Serves 4

230 g bavette or skirt steak, sliced into 8 strips
2 teaspoons curry powder
½ teaspoon coarse or flaky salt
Cooking spray
Peanut Dipping sauce:
2 tablespoons creamy peanut butter
1 tablespoon reduced-salt soy
sauce
2 teaspoons rice vinegar
1 teaspoon honey
1 teaspoon grated ginger
Special Equipment:
4 bamboo skewers, cut into halves and soaked in water for 20 minutes to keep them from burning while cooking

1. Preheat the air fryer to 182°C. Spritz the air fryer basket with cooking spray.
2. In a bowl, place the steak strips and sprinkle with the curry powder and coarse or flaky salt to season. Thread the strips onto the soaked skewers.
3. Arrange the skewers in the prepared air fryer basket and spritz with cooking spray. Air fry for 5 to 7 minutes, or until the beef is well browned, turning halfway through.
4. In the meantime, stir together the peanut butter, soy sauce, rice vinegar, honey, and ginger in a bowl to make the dipping sauce.
5. Transfer the beef to the serving dishes and let rest for 5 minutes. Serve with the peanut dipping sauce on the side.

BBQ Pork Steaks

Prep time: 5 minutes | Cook time: 15 minutes | Serves 4

4 pork steaks
1 tablespoon Cajun seasoning
2 tablespoons BBQ sauce
1 tablespoon vinegar
1 teaspoon soy sauce
120 ml brown sugar
120 ml ketchup

1. Preheat the air fryer to 143°C.
2. Sprinkle pork steaks with Cajun seasoning.
3. Combine remaining ingredients and brush onto steaks.
4. Add coated steaks to air fryer. Air fry 15 minutes until just browned.
5. Serve immediately.

Fajita Meatball Lettuce Wraps

Prep time: 10 minutes | Cook time: 10 minutes | Serves 4

450 g beef mince (85% lean)
120 ml salsa, plus more for serving if desired
60 ml chopped onions
60 ml diced green or red peppers
1 large egg, beaten
1 teaspoon fine sea salt
½ teaspoon chili powder
½ teaspoon ground cumin
1 clove garlic, minced
For Serving (Optional):
8 leaves butterhead lettuce
Pico de gallo or salsa
Lime slices

1. Spray the air fryer basket with avocado oil. Preheat the air fryer to 176°C.
2. In a large bowl, mix together all the ingredients until well combined.
3. Shape the meat mixture into eight 1-inch balls. Place the meatballs in the air fryer basket, leaving a little space between them. Air fry for 10 minutes, or until cooked through and no longer pink inside and the internal temperature reaches 64°C.
4. Serve each meatball on a lettuce leaf, topped with pico de gallo or salsa, if desired. Serve with lime slices if desired.
5. Store leftovers in an airtight container in the fridge for 3 days or in the freezer for up to a month. Reheat in a preheated 176°C air fryer for 4 minutes, or until heated through.

Smoky Pork Tenderloin

Prep time: 5 minutes | Cook time: 19 to 22 minutes | Serves 6

680 g pork tenderloin
1 tablespoon avocado oil
1 teaspoon chili powder
1 teaspoon smoked paprika

1 teaspoon garlic powder
1 teaspoon sea salt
1 teaspoon freshly ground black pepper

1. Pierce the tenderloin all over with a fork and rub the oil all over the meat.
2. In a small dish, stir together the chili powder, smoked paprika, garlic powder, salt, and pepper.
3. Rub the spice mixture all over the tenderloin.
4. Set the air fryer to 204°C. Place the pork in the air fryer basket and air fry for 10 minutes. Flip the tenderloin and cook for 9 to 12 minutes more, until an instant-read thermometer reads at least 64°C.
5. Allow the tenderloin to rest for 5 minutes, then slice and serve.

Spice-Coated Steaks with Cucumber and Snap Pea Salad

Prep time: 15 minutes | Cook time: 15 to 20 minutes | Serves 4

1 (680 g) boneless rump steak, trimmed and halved crosswise
1½ teaspoons chili powder
1½ teaspoons ground cumin
¾ teaspoon ground coriander
⅛ teaspoon cayenne pepper
⅛ teaspoon ground cinnamon
1¼ teaspoons plus ⅛ teaspoon salt, divided
½ teaspoon plus ⅛ teaspoon ground black pepper, divided
1 teaspoon plus 1½ tablespoons extra-virgin olive oil, divided

3 tablespoons mayonnaise
1½ tablespoons white wine vinegar
1 tablespoon minced fresh dill
1 small garlic clove, minced
230 g sugar snap peas, strings removed and cut in half on bias
½ cucumber, halved lengthwise and sliced thin
2 radishes, trimmed, halved and sliced thin
475 ml baby rocket

1. Preheat the air fryer to 204°C.
2. In a bowl, mix chili powder, cumin, coriander, cayenne pepper, cinnamon, 1¼ teaspoons salt and ½ teaspoon pepper until well combined.
3. Add the steaks to another bowl and pat dry with paper towels. Brush with 1 teaspoon oil and transfer to the bowl of spice mixture. Roll over to coat thoroughly.
4. Arrange the coated steaks in the air fryer basket, spaced evenly apart. Air fry for 15 to 20 minutes, or until an instant-read thermometer inserted in the thickest part of the meat registers at least 64°C. Flip halfway through to ensure even cooking.
5. Transfer the steaks to a clean work surface and wrap with aluminum foil. Let stand while preparing salad.

6. Make the salad: In a large bowl, stir together 1½ tablespoons olive oil, mayonnaise, vinegar, dill, garlic, ⅛ teaspoon salt, and ⅛ teaspoon pepper. Add snap peas, cucumber, radishes and rocket. Toss to blend well.
7. Slice the steaks and serve with the salad.

Herb-Roasted Beef Tips with Onions

Prep time: 5 minutes | Cook time: 10 minutes | Serves 4

450 g rib eye steak, cubed
2 garlic cloves, minced
2 tablespoons olive oil
1 tablespoon fresh oregano

1 teaspoon salt
½ teaspoon black pepper
1 brown onion, thinly sliced

1. Preheat the air fryer to 192°C.
2. In a medium bowl, combine the steak, garlic, olive oil, oregano, salt, pepper, and onion. Mix until all of the beef and onion are well coated.
3. Put the seasoned steak mixture into the air fryer basket. Roast for 5 minutes. Stir and roast for 5 minutes more.
4. Let rest for 5 minutes before serving with some favorite sides.

Bacon Wrapped Pork with Apple Gravy

Prep time: 10 minutes | Cook time: 25 minutes | Serves 4

Pork:
1 tablespoons Dijon mustard
1 pork tenderloin
3 strips bacon
Apple Gravy:
3 tablespoons ghee, divided

1 small shallot, chopped
2 apples
1 tablespoon almond flour
235 ml vegetable stock
½ teaspoon Dijon mustard

1. Preheat the air fryer to 182°C.
2. Spread Dijon mustard all over tenderloin and wrap with strips of bacon.
3. Put into air fryer and air fry for 12 minutes. Use a meat thermometer to check for doneness.
4. To make sauce, heat 1 tablespoons of ghee in a pan and add shallots. Cook for 1 minute.
5. Then add apples, cooking for 4 minutes until softened.
6. Add flour and 2 tablespoons of ghee to make a roux. Add stock and mustard, stirring well to combine.
7. When sauce starts to bubble, add 235 ml of sautéed apples, cooking until sauce thickens.
8. Once pork tenderloin is cooked, allow to sit 8 minutes to rest before slicing.
9. Serve topped with apple gravy.

Chapter 8 Vegetarian Mains

Chapter 8 Vegetarian Mains

Three-Cheese Courgette Boats

Prep time: 15 minutes | Cook time: 20 minutes | Serves 2

2 medium courgette
1 tablespoon avocado oil
60 ml low-carb, no-sugar-added pasta sauce
60 ml full-fat ricotta cheese
60 ml shredded Mozzarella

cheese
¼ teaspoon dried oregano
¼ teaspoon garlic powder
½ teaspoon dried parsley
2 tablespoons grated vegetarian Parmesan cheese

1.Cut off 1 inch from the top and bottom of each courgette.
2.Slice courgette in half lengthwise and use a spoon to scoop out a bit of the inside, making room for filling.
3.Brush with oil and spoon 2 tablespoons pasta sauce into each shell. In a medium bowl, mix ricotta, Mozzarella, oregano, garlic powder, and parsley. Spoon the mixture into each courgette shell.
4.Place stuffed courgette shells into the air fryer basket. Adjust the temperature to 176°C and air fry for 20 minutes.
5.To remove from the basket, use tongs or a spatula and carefully lift out.
6.Top with Parmesan. Serve immediately.

White Cheddar and Mushroom Soufflés

Prep time: 15 minutes | Cook time: 12 minutes | Serves 4

3 large eggs, whites and yolks separated
120 ml extra mature white Cheddar cheese
85 g soft white cheese

¼ teaspoon cream of tartar
¼ teaspoon salt
¼ teaspoon ground black pepper
120 ml chestnut mushrooms, sliced

1.In a large bowl, whip egg whites until stiff peaks form, about 2 minutes.
2.In a separate large bowl, beat Cheddar, egg yolks, soft white cheese, cream of tartar, salt, and pepper together until combined.
3.Fold egg whites into cheese mixture, being careful not to stir.
4.Fold in mushrooms, then pour mixture evenly into four ungreased ramekins.
5.Place ramekins into air fryer basket. Adjust the temperature to 176°C and bake for 12 minutes. Eggs will be browned on the top and firm in the centre when done.
6.Serve warm.

Spaghetti Squash Alfredo

Prep time: 10 minutes | Cook time: 15 minutes | Serves 2

½ large cooked spaghetti squash
2 tablespoons salted butter, melted
120 ml low-carb Alfredo sauce
60 ml grated vegetarian Parmesan cheese

½ teaspoon garlic powder
1 teaspoon dried parsley
¼ teaspoon ground peppercorn
120 ml shredded Italian blend cheese

1.Using a fork, remove the strands of spaghetti squash from the shell.
2.Place into a large bowl with butter and Alfredo sauce.
3.Sprinkle with Parmesan, garlic powder, parsley, and peppercorn.
4.Pour into a 1 L round baking dish and top with shredded cheese.
5.Place dish into the air fryer basket. Adjust the temperature to 160°C and bake for 15 minutes. When finished, cheese will be golden and bubbling.
6.Serve immediately.

Super Vegetable Burger

Prep time: 15 minutes | Cook time: 12 minutes | Serves 8

230 g cauliflower, steamed and diced, rinsed and drained
2 teaspoons coconut oil, melted
2 teaspoons minced garlic
60 ml desiccated coconut
120 ml oats
3 tablespoons flour
1 tablespoon flaxseeds plus 3

tablespoons water, divided
1 teaspoon mustard powder
2 teaspoons thyme
2 teaspoons parsley
2 teaspoons chives
Salt and ground black pepper, to taste
235 ml breadcrumbs

1.Preheat the air fryer to 200°C.
2.Combine the cauliflower with all the ingredients, except for the breadcrumbs, incorporating everything well.
3.Using the hands, shape 8 equal-sized amounts of the mixture into burger patties.
4.Coat the patties in breadcrumbs before putting them in the air fryer basket in a single layer.
5.Air fry for 12 minutes or until crispy.
6.Serve hot.

Gold Ravioli

Prep time: 10 minutes | Cook time: 6 minutes | Serves 4

120 ml panko breadcrumbs
2 teaspoons Engevita yeast flakes
1 teaspoon dried basil
1 teaspoon dried oregano
1 teaspoon garlic powder

Salt and ground black pepper, to taste
60 ml aquafaba or egg alternative
227 g ravioli
Cooking spray

1. Cover the air fryer basket with aluminium foil and coat with a light brushing of oil.
2. Preheat the air fryer to 204°C.
3. Combine the panko breadcrumbs, Engevita yeast flakes, basil, oregano, and garlic powder.
4. Sprinkle with salt and pepper to taste.
5. Put the aquafaba in a separate bowl.
6. Dip the ravioli in the aquafaba before coating it in the panko mixture.
7. Spritz with cooking spray and transfer to the air fryer.
8. Air fry for 6 minutes. Shake the air fryer basket halfway.
9. Serve hot.

Sweet Potatoes with Courgette

Prep time: 20 minutes | Cook time: 20 minutes | Serves 4

2 large-sized sweet potatoes, peeled and quartered
1 medium courgette, sliced
1 Serrano or jalapeño pepper, deseeded and thinly sliced
1 pepper, deseeded and thinly sliced
1 to 2 carrots, cut into matchsticks
60 ml olive oil

1½ tablespoons maple syrup
½ teaspoon porcini powder or paste
¼ teaspoon mustard powder
½ teaspoon fennel seeds
1 tablespoon garlic powder
½ teaspoon fine sea salt
¼ teaspoon ground black pepper
Tomato ketchup, for serving

1. Put the sweet potatoes, courgette, peppers, and the carrot into the air fryer basket. Coat with a drizzling of olive oil.
2. Preheat the air fryer to 176°C. Air fry the vegetables for 15 minutes.
3. In the meantime, prepare the sauce by vigorously combining the other ingredients, except for the tomato ketchup, with a whisk.
4. Lightly grease a baking dish. Transfer the cooked vegetables to the baking dish, pour over the sauce and coat the vegetables well.
5. Increase the temperature to 200°C and air fry the vegetables for an additional 5 minutes.
6. Serve warm with a side of ketchup.

Parmesan Artichokes

Prep time: 10 minutes | Cook time: 10 minutes | Serves 4

2 medium artichokes, trimmed and quartered, centre removed
2 tablespoons coconut oil
1 large egg, beaten
120 ml grated vegetarian

Parmesan cheese
60 ml blanched finely ground almond flour
½ teaspoon crushed red pepper flakes

1. In a large bowl, toss artichokes in coconut oil and then dip each piece into the egg.
2. Mix the Parmesan and almond flour in a large bowl.
3. Add artichoke pieces and toss to cover as completely as possible, sprinkle with pepper flakes.
4. Place into the air fryer basket. Adjust the temperature to 204°C and air fry for 10 minutes. Toss the basket two times during cooking.
5. Serve warm.

Buffalo Cauliflower Bites with Blue Cheese

Prep time: 10 minutes | Cook time: 8 to 10 minutes | Serves 4

1 large head cauliflower, chopped into florets
1 tablespoon olive oil
Salt and freshly ground black pepper, to taste
60 ml unsalted butter, melted
60 ml hot sauce
Garlic Blue Cheese Dip:

120 ml mayonnaise
60 ml sour cream
2 tablespoons double cream
1 tablespoon fresh lemon juice
1 clove garlic, minced
60 ml crumbled blue cheese
Salt and freshly ground black pepper, to taste

1. Preheat the air fryer to 204°C.
2. In a large bowl, combine the cauliflower and olive oil. Season to taste with salt and black pepper. Toss until the vegetables are thoroughly coated.
3. Working in batches, place half of the cauliflower in the air fryer basket.
4. Pausing halfway through the cooking time to shake the basket, air fry for 8 to 10 minutes until the cauliflower is evenly browned.
5. Transfer to a large bowl and repeat with the remaining cauliflower. In a small bowl, whisk together the melted butter and hot sauce.
6. To make the dip: In a small bowl, combine the mayonnaise, sour cream, double cream, lemon juice, garlic, and blue cheese.
7. Season to taste with salt and freshly ground black pepper.
8. Just before serving, pour the butter mixture over the cauliflower and toss gently until thoroughly coated.
9. Serve with the dip on the side.

Broccoli-Cheese Fritters

Prep time: 5 minutes | Cook time: 20 to 25 minutes | Serves 4

235 ml broccoli florets
235 ml shredded Mozzarella cheese
180 ml almond flour
120 ml milled flaxseed, divided
2 teaspoons baking powder

1 teaspoon garlic powder
Salt and freshly ground black pepper, to taste
2 eggs, lightly beaten
120 ml ranch dressing

1. Preheat the air fryer to 204°C.
2. In a food processor fitted with a metal blade, pulse the broccoli until very finely chopped.
3. Transfer the broccoli to a large bowl and add the Mozzarella, almond flour, 60 ml milled flaxseed, baking powder, and garlic powder. Stir until thoroughly combined.
4. Season to taste with salt and black pepper. Add the eggs and stir again to form a sticky dough. Shape the dough into 1¼-inch fritters.
5. Place the remaining 60 ml milled flaxseed in a shallow bowl and roll the fritters in the meal to form an even coating.
6. Working in batches if necessary, arrange the fritters in a single layer in the basket of the air fryer and spray generously with olive oil. Pausing halfway through the cooking time to shake the basket, air fry for 20 to 25 minutes until the fritters are golden brown and crispy.
7. Serve with the ranch dressing for dipping.

Greek Stuffed Aubergine

Prep time: 15 minutes | Cook time: 20 minutes | Serves 2

1 large aubergine
2 tablespoons unsalted butter
¼ medium brown onion, diced
60 ml chopped artichoke hearts

235 ml fresh spinach
2 tablespoons diced red pepper
120 ml crumbled feta

1. Slice aubergine in half lengthwise and scoop out flesh, leaving enough inside for shell to remain intact.
2. Take aubergine that was scooped out, chop it, and set aside.
3. In a medium skillet over medium heat, add butter and onion. Sauté until onions begin to soften, about 3 to 5 minutes.
4. Add chopped aubergine, artichokes, spinach, and pepper. Continue cooking 5 minutes until peppers soften and spinach wilts.
5. Remove from the heat and gently fold in the feta.
6. Place filling into each aubergine shell and place into the air fryer basket.
7. Adjust the temperature to 160°C and air fry for 20 minutes. Aubergine will be tender when done.
8. Serve warm.

Pesto Vegetable Skewers

Prep time: 30 minutes | Cook time: 8 minutes | Makes 8 skewers

1 medium courgette, trimmed and cut into ½-inch slices
½ medium brown onion, peeled and cut into 1-inch squares
1 medium red pepper, seeded and cut into 1-inch squares

16 whole cremini or chestnut mushrooms
80 ml basil pesto
½ teaspoon salt
¼ teaspoon ground black pepper

1. Divide courgette slices, onion, and pepper into eight even portions.
2. Place on 6-inch skewers for a total of eight kebabs.
3. Add 2 mushrooms to each skewer and brush kebabs generously with pesto.
4. Sprinkle each kebab with salt and black pepper on all sides, then place into ungreased air fryer basket.
5. Adjust the temperature to 192°C and air fry for 8 minutes, turning kebabs halfway through cooking. Vegetables will be browned at the edges and tender-crisp when done.
6. Serve warm.

Fried Root Vegetable Medley with Thyme

Prep time: 10 minutes | Cook time: 22 minutes | Serves 4

2 carrots, sliced
2 potatoes, cut into chunks
1 swede, cut into chunks
1 turnip, cut into chunks
1 beetroot, cut into chunks
8 shallots, halved

2 tablespoons olive oil
Salt and black pepper, to taste
2 tablespoons tomato pesto
2 tablespoons water
2 tablespoons chopped fresh thyme

1. Preheat the air fryer to 204°C.
2. Toss the carrots, potatoes, swede, turnip, beetroot, shallots, olive oil, salt, and pepper in a large mixing bowl until the root vegetables are evenly coated.
3. Place the root vegetables in the air fryer basket and air fry for 12 minutes.
4. Shake the basket and air fry for another 10 minutes until they are cooked to your preferred doneness.
5. Meanwhile, in a small bowl, whisk together the tomato pesto and water until smooth.
6. When ready, remove the root vegetables from the basket to a platter.
7. Drizzle with the tomato pesto mixture and sprinkle with the thyme. Serve immediately.

Crispy Fried Okra with Chilli

Prep time: 5 minutes | Cook time: 10 minutes | Serves 4

3 tablespoons sour cream

2 tablespoons flour

2 tablespoons semolina

½ teaspoon red chilli powder

Salt and black pepper, to taste

450 g okra, halved

Cooking spray

1.Preheat the air fryer to 204°C.

2.Spray the air fryer basket with cooking spray.

3.In a shallow bowl, place the sour cream.

4.In another shallow bowl, thoroughly combine the flour, semolina, red chilli powder, salt, and pepper.

5.Dredge the okra in the sour cream, then roll in the flour mixture until evenly coated.

6.Arrange the okra in the air fryer basket and air fry for 10 minutes, flipping the okra halfway through, or until golden brown and crispy.

7.Cool for 5 minutes before serving.

Sweet Pepper Nachos

Prep time: 10 minutes | Cook time: 5 minutes | Serves 2

6 mini sweet peppers, seeded and sliced in half

180 ml shredded Colby jack or Monterey Jack cheese

60 ml sliced pickled jalapeños

½ medium avocado, peeled, pitted, and diced

2 tablespoons sour cream

1.Place peppers into an ungreased round non-stick baking dish. Sprinkle with cheese and top with jalapeños.

2.Place dish into air fryer basket. Adjust the temperature to 176°C and bake for 5 minutes. Cheese will be melted and bubbly when done.

3.Remove dish from air fryer and top with avocado. Drizzle with sour cream.

4.Serve warm.

Black Bean and Tomato Chilli

Prep time: 15 minutes | Cook time: 23 minutes | Serves 6

1 tablespoon olive oil

1 medium onion, diced

3 garlic cloves, minced

235 ml vegetable broth

3 cans black beans, drained and rinsed

2 cans diced tomatoes

2 chipotle peppers, chopped

2 teaspoons cumin

2 teaspoons chilli powder

1 teaspoon dried oregano

½ teaspoon salt

1.Over a medium heat, fry the garlic and onions in the olive oil for

3 minutes.

2.Add the remaining ingredients, stirring constantly and scraping the bottom to prevent sticking.

3.Preheat the air fryer to 204°C.

4.Take a dish and place the mixture inside.

5.Put a sheet of aluminium foil on top.

6.Transfer to the air fryer and bake for 20 minutes.

7.When ready, plate up and serve immediately.

Cheesy Cauliflower Pizza Crust

Prep time: 15 minutes | Cook time: 11 minutes | Serves 2

1 (340 g) steamer bag cauliflower

120 ml shredded extra mature Cheddar cheese

1 large egg

2 tablespoons blanched finely ground almond flour

1 teaspoon Italian blend seasoning

1.Cook cauliflower according to package instructions.

2.Remove from bag and place into cheesecloth or paper towel to remove excess water.

3.Place cauliflower into a large bowl. Add cheese, egg, almond flour, and Italian seasoning to the bowl and mix well.

4.Cut a piece of parchment to fit your air fryer basket. Press cauliflower into 6-inch round circle.

5.Place into the air fryer basket. Adjust the temperature to 182°C and air fry for 11 minutes. After 7 minutes, flip the pizza crust.

6.Add preferred toppings to pizza. Place back into air fryer basket and cook an additional 4 minutes or until fully cooked and golden.

7.Serve immediately.

Cheese Stuffed Peppers

Prep time: 20 minutes | Cook time: 15 minutes | Serves 2

1 red pepper, top and seeds removed

1 yellow pepper, top and seeds removed

Salt and pepper, to taste

235 ml Cottage cheese

4 tablespoons mayonnaise

2 pickles, chopped

1.Arrange the peppers in the lightly greased air fryer basket.

2.Cook in the preheated air fryer at 204°C for 15 minutes, turning them over halfway through the cooking time. Season with salt and pepper.

3.Then, in a mixing bowl, combine the soft white cheese with the mayonnaise and chopped pickles.

4.Stuff the pepper with the soft white cheese mixture and serve. Enjoy!

Rice and Aubergine Bowl

Prep time: 15 minutes | Cook time: 10 minutes | Serves 4

60 ml sliced cucumber

1 teaspoon salt

1 tablespoon sugar

7 tablespoons Japanese rice vinegar

3 medium aubergines, sliced

3 tablespoons sweet white miso paste

1 tablespoon mirin rice wine

1 L cooked sushi rice

4 spring onions

1 tablespoon toasted sesame seeds

1. Coat the cucumber slices with the rice wine vinegar, salt, and sugar.
2. Put a dish on top of the bowl to weight it down completely.
3. In a bowl, mix the aubergines, mirin rice wine, and miso paste. Allow to marinate for half an hour.
4. Preheat the air fryer to 204°C. Put the aubergine slices in the air fryer and air fry for 10 minutes.
5. Fill the bottom of a serving bowl with rice and top with the aubergines and pickled cucumbers.
6. Add the spring onions and sesame seeds for garnish.
7. Serve immediately.

Mediterranean Pan Pizza

Prep time: 5 minutes | Cook time: 8 minutes | Serves 2

235 ml shredded Mozzarella cheese

¼ medium red pepper, seeded and chopped

120 ml chopped fresh spinach leaves

2 tablespoons chopped black olives

2 tablespoons crumbled feta cheese

1. Sprinkle Mozzarella into an ungreased round non-stick baking dish in an even layer.
2. Add remaining ingredients on top. Place dish into air fryer basket.
3. Adjust the temperature to 176°C and bake for 8 minutes, checking halfway through to avoid burning. Top of pizza will be golden brown, and the cheese melted when done.
4. Remove dish from fryer and let cool 5 minutes before slicing and serving.

Spinach Cheese Casserole

Prep time: 15 minutes | Cook time: 15 minutes | Serves 4

1 tablespoon salted butter, melted

60 ml diced brown onion

227 g full fat soft white cheese

80 ml full-fat mayonnaise

80 ml full-fat sour cream

60 ml chopped pickled jalapeños

475 ml fresh spinach, chopped

475 ml cauliflower florets, chopped

235 ml artichoke hearts, chopped

1. In a large bowl, mix butter, onion, soft white cheese, mayonnaise, and sour cream.
2. Fold in jalapeños, spinach, cauliflower, and artichokes. Pour the mixture into a round baking dish.
3. Cover with foil and place into the air fryer basket. Adjust the temperature to 188°C and set the timer for 15 minutes. In the last 2 minutes of cooking, remove the foil to brown the top.
4. Serve warm.

Chapter 9 Desserts

Chapter 9 Desserts

Gingerbread

Prep time: 5 minutes | Cook time: 20 minutes | Makes 1 loaf

Cooking spray
125 g plain flour
2 tablespoons granulated sugar
¾ teaspoon ground ginger
¼ teaspoon cinnamon
1 teaspoon baking powder
½ teaspoon baking soda
⅛ teaspoon salt
1 egg
70 g treacle
120 ml buttermilk
2 tablespoons coconut, or avocado oil
1 teaspoon pure vanilla extract

1. Preheat the air fryer to 164°C.
2. Spray a baking dish lightly with cooking spray.
3. In a medium bowl, mix together all the dry ingredients.
4. In a separate bowl, beat the egg. Add treacle, buttermilk, oil, and vanilla and stir until well mixed.
5. Pour liquid mixture into dry ingredients and stir until well blended.
6. Pour batter into baking dish and bake for 20 minutes, or until toothpick inserted in center of loaf comes out clean.

Strawberry Scone Shortcake

Prep time: 10 minutes | Cook time: 20 minutes | Serves 4 to 6

165 g plain flour
3 tablespoons granulated sugar
1½ teaspoons baking powder
1 teaspoon kosher, or coarse sea salt
8 tablespoons unsalted butter, cubed and chilled
315 ml heavy cream, chilled
Turbinado (raw cane) sugar, for sprinkling
2 tablespoons icing sugar, plus more for dusting
½ teaspoon vanilla extract
165 g quartered fresh strawberries

1. In a large bowl, whisk together the flour, granulated sugar, baking powder, and salt. Add the butter and use your fingers to break apart the butter pieces while working them into the flour mixture, until pea-size pieces form. Pour 155 ml of the cream over the flour mixture and, using a rubber spatula, mix the ingredients together until just combined.
2. Transfer the dough to a work surface and form into a 7-inch-wide disk. Brush the top with water, then sprinkle with some turbinado sugar. Using a large metal spatula, transfer the dough to the air fryer and bake at 176°C until golden brown and fluffy, about 20 minutes. Let cool in the air fryer basket for 5 minutes, then turn out onto a wire rack, right-side up, to cool completely.
3. Meanwhile, in a bowl, beat the remaining 155 ml of cream, the icing sugar, and vanilla until stiff peaks form. Split the scone like a hamburger bun and spread the strawberries over the bottom. Top with the whipped cream and cover with the top of the scone. Dust with icing sugar and cut into wedges to serve.

Butter Flax Cookies

Prep time: 25 minutes | Cook time: 20 minutes | Serves 4

225 g almond meal
2 tablespoons flaxseed meal
30 g monk fruit, or equivalent sweetener
1 teaspoon baking powder
A pinch of grated nutmeg
A pinch of coarse salt
1 large egg, room temperature.
110 g unsalted butter, room temperature
1 teaspoon vanilla extract

1. Mix the almond meal, flaxseed meal, monk fruit, baking powder, grated nutmeg, and salt in a bowl.
2. In a separate bowl, whisk the egg, butter, and vanilla extract.
3. Stir the egg mixture into dry mixture; mix to combine well or until it forms a nice, soft dough.
4. Roll your dough out and cut out with a cookie cutter of your choice. Bake in the preheated air fryer at 176°C for 10 minutes. Decrease the temperature to 164°C and cook for 10 minutes longer. Bon appétit!

Vanilla Scones

Prep time: 20 minutes | Cook time: 10 minutes | Serves 6

110 g coconut flour
½ teaspoon baking powder
1 teaspoon apple cider vinegar
2 teaspoons mascarpone
60 ml heavy cream
1 teaspoon vanilla extract
1 tablespoon granulated sweetener
Cooking spray

1. In the mixing bowl, mix coconut flour with baking powder, apple cider vinegar, mascarpone, heavy cream, vanilla extract, and sweetener.
2. Knead the dough and cut into scones.
3. Then put them in the air fryer basket and sprinkle with cooking spray.
4. Cook the vanilla scones at 185°C for 10 minutes.

Chocolate Bread Pudding

Prep time: 10 minutes | Cook time: 10 to 12 minutes | Serves 4

Nonstick, flour-infused baking spray	2 tablespoons cocoa powder
1 egg	3 tablespoons light brown sugar
1 egg yolk	3 tablespoons peanut butter
175 ml chocolate milk	1 teaspoon vanilla extract
	5 slices firm white bread, cubed

1. Spray a 6-by-2-inch round baking pan with the baking spray. Set aside.
2. In a medium bowl, whisk the egg, egg yolk, chocolate milk, cocoa powder, brown sugar, peanut butter, and vanilla until thoroughly combined. Stir in the bread cubes and let soak for 10 minutes. Spoon this mixture into the prepared pan.
3. Insert the crisper plate into the basket and the basket into the unit. Preheat the unit to 164ºC.
4. cook the pudding for about 10 minutes and then check if done. It is done when it is firm to the touch. If not, resume cooking.
5. When the cooking is complete, let the pudding cool for 5 minutes. Serve warm.

Caramelized Fruit Skewers

Prep time: 10 minutes | Cook time: 3 to 5 minutes | Serves 4

2 peaches, peeled, pitted, and thickly sliced	½ teaspoon ground cinnamon
3 plums, halved and pitted	¼ teaspoon ground allspice
3 nectarines, halved and pitted	Pinch cayenne pepper
1 tablespoon honey	Special Equipment:
	8 metal skewers

1. Preheat the air fryer to 204ºC.
2. Thread, alternating peaches, plums, and nectarines, onto the metal skewers that fit into the air fryer.
3. Thoroughly combine the honey, cinnamon, allspice, and cayenne in a small bowl. Brush the glaze generously over the fruit skewers.
4. Transfer the fruit skewers to the air fryer basket. You may need to cook in batches to avoid overcrowding.
5. Air fry for 3 to 5 minutes, or until the fruit is caramelized.
6. Remove from the basket and repeat with the remaining fruit skewers.
7. Let the fruit skewers rest for 5 minutes before serving.

Funnel Cake

Prep time: 10 minutes | Cook time: 5 minutes | Serves 4

Coconut, or avocado oil, for spraying	240 ml fat-free vanilla Greek yogurt
110 g self-raising flour, plus more for dusting	½ teaspoon ground cinnamon
	¼ cup icing sugar

1. Preheat the air fryer to 192ºC. Line the air fryer basket with baking paper, and spray lightly with oil.
2. In a large bowl, mix together the flour, yogurt and cinnamon until the mixture forms a ball.
3. Place the dough on a lightly floured work surface and knead for about 2 minutes.
4. Cut the dough into 4 equal pieces, then cut each of those into 6 pieces. You should have 24 pieces in total.
5. Roll the pieces into 8- to 10-inch-long ropes. Loosely mound the ropes into 4 piles of 6 ropes.
6. Place the dough piles in the prepared basket, and spray liberally with oil. You may need to work in batches, depending on the size of your air fryer.
7. Cook for 5 minutes, or until lightly browned.
8. Dust with the icing sugar before serving.

Almond Butter Cookie Balls

Prep time: 5 minutes | Cook time: 10 minutes | Makes 10 balls

70 g almond butter	25 g desiccated unsweetened coconut
1 large egg	
1 teaspoon vanilla extract	40 g low-carb, sugar-free chocolate chips
30 g low-carb protein powder	
30 g powdered sweetener	½ teaspoon ground cinnamon

1. In a large bowl, mix almond butter and egg. Add in vanilla, protein powder, and sweetener.
2. Fold in coconut, chocolate chips, and cinnamon. Roll into 1-inch balls. Place balls into a round baking pan and put into the air fryer basket.
3. Adjust the temperature to 160ºC and bake for 10 minutes.
4. Allow to cool completely. Store in an airtight container in the refrigerator up to 4 days.

S'mores

Prep time: 5 minutes | Cook time: 30 seconds | Makes 8 s'mores

Coconut, or avocado oil, for spraying	2 (45 g) chocolate bars
8 digestive biscuits	4 large marshmallows

1. Line the air fryer basket with baking paper and spray lightly with oil.
2. Place 4 biscuits into the prepared basket.
3. Break the chocolate bars in half, and place 1/2 on top of each biscuit. Top with 1 marshmallow.
4. Air fry at 188ºC for 30 seconds, or until the marshmallows are puffed, golden brown and slightly melted.
5. Top with the remaining biscuits and serve.

Lush Chocolate Chip Cookies

Prep time: 7 minutes | Cook time: 9 minutes | Serves 4

3 tablespoons butter, at room temperature	chocolate
	¼ teaspoon baking soda
65 g light brown sugar, plus 1 tablespoon	½ teaspoon vanilla extract
	120 g semisweet chocolate
1 egg yolk	chips
70 g plain flour	Nonstick flour-infused baking
2 tablespoons ground white	spray

1. In medium bowl, beat together the butter and brown sugar until fluffy. Stir in the egg yolk.
2. Add the flour, white chocolate, baking soda, and vanilla and mix well. Stir in the chocolate chips.
3. Line a 6-by-2-inch round baking pan with baking paper. Spray the baking paper with flour-infused baking spray.
4. Insert the crisper plate into the basket and the basket into the unit. Preheat the unit to 148°C.
5. Spread the batter into the prepared pan, leaving a ½-inch border on all sides.
6. Once the unit is preheated, place the pan into the basket.
7. Bake to cookies for 9 minutes.
8. When the cooking is complete, the cookies should be light brown and just barely set. Remove the pan from the basket and let cool for 10 minutes. Remove the cookie from the pan, remove the baking paper, and let cool completely on a wire rack.

Apple Hand Pies

Prep time: 15 minutes | Cook time: 25 minutes | Serves 8

2 apples, cored and diced	2 teaspoons cornflour
60 ml honey	1 teaspoon water
1 teaspoon ground cinnamon	1 sheet shortcrust pastry cut into
1 teaspoon vanilla extract	4
⅛ teaspoon ground nutmeg	Cooking oil spray

1. Insert the crisper plate into the basket and the basket into the unit. Preheat the unit to 204°C.
2. In a metal bowl that fits into the basket, stir together the apples, honey, cinnamon, vanilla, and nutmeg.
3. In a small bowl, whisk the cornflour and water until the cornflour dissolves.
4. Once the unit is preheated, place the metal bowl with the apples into the basket.
5. cook for 2 minutes then stir the apples. Resume cooking for 2 minutes.
6. Remove the bowl and stir the cornflour mixture into the apples.

Reinsert the metal bowl into the basket and resume cooking for about 30 minutes until the sauce thickens slightly.
7. When the cooking is complete, refrigerate the apples while you prepare the piecrust.
8. Cut each piecrust into 2 (4-inch) circles. You should have 8 circles of crust.
9. Lay the piecrusts on a work surface. Divide the apple filling among the piecrusts, mounding the mixture in the center of each round.
10. Fold each piecrust over so the top layer of crust is about an inch short of the bottom layer. (The edges should not meet.) Use the back of a fork to seal the edges.
11. Insert the crisper plate into the basket and the basket into the unit. Preheat the unit 204°C again.
12. Once the unit is preheated, spray the crisper plate with cooking oil, line the basket with baking paper, and spray it with cooking oil. Working in batches, place the hand pies into the basket in a single layer.
13. Cook the pies for 10 minutes.
14. When the cooking is complete, let the hand pies cool for 5 minutes before removing from the basket. 16. Repeat steps 12, 13, and 14 with the remaining pies.

Lemon Raspberry Muffins

Prep time: 5 minutes | Cook time: 15 minutes | Serves 6

220 g almond flour	¼ teaspoon salt
75 g powdered sweetener	2 eggs
1¼ teaspoons baking powder	240 ml sour cream
⅓ teaspoon ground allspice	120 ml coconut oil
⅓ teaspoon ground star anise	60 g raspberries
½ teaspoon grated lemon zest	

1. Preheat the air fryer to 176°C. Line a muffin pan with 6 paper cases.
2. In a mixing bowl, mix the almond flour, sweetener, baking powder, allspice, star anise, lemon zest, and salt.
3. In another mixing bowl, beat the eggs, sour cream, and coconut oil until well mixed. Add the egg mixture to the flour mixture and stir to combine. Mix in the raspberries.
4. Scrape the batter into the prepared muffin cups, filling each about three-quarters full.
5. Bake for 15 minutes, or until the tops are golden and a toothpick inserted in the middle comes out clean.
6. Allow the muffins to cool for 10 minutes in the muffin pan before removing and serving.

Coconut Muffins

Prep time: 5 minutes | Cook time: 25 minutes | Serves 5

55 g coconut flour	1 teaspoon baking powder
2 tablespoons cocoa powder	2 tablespoons coconut oil
3 tablespoons granulated sweetener	2 eggs, beaten
	50 g desiccated coconut

1. In the mixing bowl, mix all ingredients.
2. Then pour the mixture into the molds of the muffin and transfer in the air fryer basket.
3. Cook the muffins at 176°C for 25 minutes.

Almond-Roasted Pears

Prep time: 10 minutes | Cook time: 15 to 20 minutes | Serves 4

Yogurt Topping:	2 whole pears
140-170 g pot vanilla Greek yogurt	4 crushed Biscoff biscuits
¼ teaspoon almond flavoring	1 tablespoon flaked almonds
	1 tablespoon unsalted butter

1. Stir the almond flavoring into yogurt and set aside while preparing pears.
2. Halve each pear and spoon out the core.
3. Place pear halves in air fryer basket, skin side down.
4. Stir together the crushed biscuits and almonds. Place a quarter of this mixture into the hollow of each pear half.
5. Cut butter into 4 pieces and place one piece on top of biscuit mixture in each pear.
6. Roast at 184°C for 15 to 20 minutes, or until pears have cooked through but are still slightly firm.
7. Serve pears warm with a dollop of yogurt topping.

Mixed Berry Hand Pies

Prep time: 5 minutes | Cook time: 30 minutes | Serves 4

150 g granulated sugar	two equal portions
½ teaspoon ground cinnamon	1 teaspoon water
1 tablespoon cornflour	1 package refrigerated shortcrust
150 g blueberries	pastry (or your own homemade
150 g blackberries	pastry)
150 g raspberries, divided into	1 egg, beaten

1. Combine the sugar, cinnamon, and cornstarch in a small saucepan. Add the blueberries, blackberries, and ½ of the raspberries. Toss the berries gently to coat them evenly. Add the teaspoon of water to the saucepan and turn the stovetop on to medium-high heat, stirring occasionally. Once the berries break down, release their juice, and start to simmer (about 5 minutes), simmer for another couple of minutes and then transfer the mixture to a bowl, stir in the remaining ½ of the raspberries and let it cool.
2. Preheat the air fryer to 188°C.
3. Cut the pie dough into four 5-inch circles and four 6-inch circles.
4. Spread the 6-inch circles on a flat surface. Divide the berry filling between all four circles. Brush the perimeter of the dough circles with a little water. Place the 5-inch circles on top of the filling and press the perimeter of the dough circles together to seal. Roll the edges of the bottom circle up over the top circle to make a crust around the filling. Press a fork around the crust to make decorative indentations and to seal the crust shut. Brush the pies with egg wash and sprinkle a little sugar on top. Poke a small hole in the center of each pie with a paring knife to vent the dough.
5. Air fry two pies at a time. Brush or spray the air fryer basket with oil and place the pies into the basket. Air fry for 9 minutes. Turn the pies over and air fry for another 6 minutes. Serve warm or at room temperature.

Printed in Great Britain
by Amazon

10873898R00038